W9-BCP-362

The Radical Leap

The Radical Leap

A Personal Lesson in Extreme Leadership

Steve Farber

Radical Leap: A Personal Lesson in Extreme Leadership

ISBN: 9780989300216

For information on distribution rights, royalties, derivative works or licensing opportunities on behalf of this content or work, please contact Mission Boulevard Press and Digital below or via email, info@missionboulevardpress.com.

COMPANIES, ORGANIZATIONS, INSTITUTIONS, AND INDUSTRY PUBLICATIONS: Quantity discounts are available on bulk purchases of this book for reselling, educational purposes, subscription incentives, gifts, sponsorship, or fundraising. Special books or book excerpts can also be created to fit specific needs such as private labeling with your logo on the cover and a message from a VIP printed inside. Contact veronica@missionboulevardpress.com or call 858-513-4184.

Mission Boulevard Press and Digital
1501 India Street, Suite 103-86 San Diego, CA 92101
info@missionboulevardpress.com

This book was printed in the United States of America.

Cover design: Joy Stauber
Book interior design: Abbey Gaterud
Surfer illustration: Design Solutions
Photo illustration: Lizzie Callen
Photo: Veer

Book set in Warnock Pro.

I dedicate this book to the ever-expanding
community of Extreme Leadership
Practitioners and Facilitators around the world.

Thank you for giving me the opportunity
to do what I love in the service of
people who love what I do.

Also by Steve Farber

The Radical Edge
Greater Than Yourself
Love Is Just Damn Good Business

Money can buy you a fine dog, but only love can make him wag his tail.
— Kinky Friedman

CONTENTS

Introduction to the 2019 Edition

15 years ago, on a warm San Diego day in April, I took my first step into the world of publishing when *The Radical Leap: A Personal Lesson in Extreme Leadership* shipped to bookstores (remember those?) and online outlets around the US.

My deep, dark, secret fear at the time of *Leap's* debut was that the title was overblown, that the content of the book wouldn't live up to its name, that it wouldn't be *radical* enough.

After all, weren't the elements of Love, Energy, Audacity, and Proof obvious, self-evident, leadership traits?

Apparently not.

The central idea in this little book—that we should all strive to "do what we love in the service of people who love what we do"—has been, for many people over the last decade and a half, a truly radical, transformational, life-altering idea. And not just at work. And even though the business and social landscape is very different today than it was in 2004, the practice of LEAP remains a consistent source of ideas, inspiration and action for many people in all walks of life and all aspects of business. And, some would argue, it's even more important, vibrant and relevant today.

In the decade since *Leap's* first publication, I've not only heard from corporate businesspeople and entrepreneurs, but also from principals, schoolteachers and students; pastors, rabbis and clergy people of all stripes; bloggers and social media mavens; volunteer workers and nonprofit missionaries, who've reached out to me to say that the ideas and inspiration in this book have helped them excel as leaders and succeed in changing their pieces of the world for the better. And several of these people—I'm grateful to say—I now count among my dearest friends.

For many, it turns out that *The Radical Leap* was pretty radical after all.

I invite you to dive in and find out for yourself.

This book is a novel. A parable, of sorts. It will take you a short time to read these pages and a lifetime to practice the ideas herein. But if you do, my hope is that you'll become the walking, talking, living, breathing example of Extreme Leadership in action.

And to help you get there, at the end of the book I've included *Your Radical Leap: A Self-Assessment for Extreme Leaders* for you to use as a mirror, as it were, into your own behaviors. If you rate yourself with a hefty dose of honesty and candor, I think you'll find that it will be a very helpful developmental tool.

As my friend and mentor, Jim Kouzes, is fond of saying, "Leadership development is self development."

By holding ourselves accountable to our own individual and collective growth, we will have a real shot at changing the world for the better—for the next 15 years and beyond.

— Steve Farber, San Diego, California

Introduction to the Original Edition

Business parables are popular, and chances are you've gobbled up a few. You've managed for a minute, let's say, or moved your cheese. You've fished, gone gung-ho, and created raving fans. Well, I reluctantly admit that I've read my share as well. "Reluctantly" may seem like an odd comment coming from the author of the book you now hold in your hands, but my hope is that reading this book will be a different experience—that this story will stand out from the parable pack. I wanted to write something a little...well...grittier. A little funkier, maybe. Something with snap and humor and insight all in the same package. Something that will genuinely entertain you while it helps you transform your business and your leadership abilities. Not to mention something with a healthy dose of humility.

The characters you're about to meet are "crossbreeds" of my experience and my imagination. They represent the people I've met, the teachers I've had, and the clients I've worked with over the past decade and a half. Some scenes are true and accurate depictions of actual events; some have been just plain fabricated from my twitching gray matter. I'm not going to say which are which, but I suspect you'd be surprised if you knew the answer. The principles, however, are as real, as important, and as crucial as anything you'll find in the most scholarly of tomes. Maybe—dare I say it—even more so.

I invite you to start at the beginning and cruise all the way through to the final pages. It won't take long: a plane ride, maybe, or a couple of lunch breaks. And ultimately, when you get to the end, I invite you to take up the challenge of Extreme Leadership. At the very least, I hope you enjoy the reading as much as I enjoyed the writing.

The Radical Leap

A Personal Lesson in Extreme Leadership

Tuesday

1.

In one respect, at least, I'm a creature of habit. Every day I'm in town, I head for the waterfront. Which is why, I realize now, it had been easy for him to find me.

It was another one of those typical San Diego days, the sky was blue and bright, and the ocean was sparkling as it slapped its waves onto the shores of Mission Beach. I was sitting on the seawall and watching the scenery walk, run, skate, and cycle by on the boardwalk. Here was the epitome of beach culture, beautifully sculpted people gathered together for the top-end of the gene pool convention. This world, with its high tattoo and body piercing to square inch of flesh ratio, was very different from the corporate world I, as a leadership consultant, worked in every day. That's why I loved living here, it kept me lively. I lifted my face to the sun, closed my eyes behind my Maui Jim shades, and felt the stress being sucked out through my pores.

A young woman's voice broke the spell: "Excuse me, sir, may I ask you a question?" She was around twenty-two, blonde, of course, and wore a bikini. None of that was unusual in this neighborhood. Her clipboard was unusual, though, as was the stack of three-by-five papers in her hand.

"I suppose so...Depends on what the question is," I said, feeling a bit hopeful that I was about to enter into a classic middle-aged male fantasy scenario, if you know what I mean.

"I'm doing a study for my business class at USD so I've been polling people here on the beach," she waved her stack of papers.

"And the question is..." I prompted, feeling the fantasy fade.

"What is leadership?" she asked.

A feeling of chilling synchronicity swept over me. I explained to this sun-worshiping surveyor that this was exactly the question I helped people answer every day for a living; that I had worked at one of America's top leadership development firms, The Tom Peters Company, for many years, and that it would take me at least a week and a lot more than a five-inch rectangle of paper to even begin to try to answer that question in a meaningful way. Still, I felt compelled to participate.

I'd heard a wide variety of businesspeople describe leadership; I'd heard consultants describe leadership; and I'd heard the gray-haired, pantsuit-and-pumps crowd describe leadership. What I'd never heard was a description from a tongue-pierced, tattooed skater or a bikini-clad rollerblader. Here I was, in the heart of San Diego slacker culture, and suddenly I was dying of curiosity to know what these people on the beach had to say.

"Listen," I said, "I'll make you a deal. I'll write you a definition of leadership straight from the management gurus if you'll show me all of the other responses you've gotten so far."

She readily agreed, so I wrote a line from Jim Kouzes and Barry Posner's book, *The Leadership Challenge*: "Leadership is the art of mobilizing others to want to struggle for shared aspirations." It's a great definition, and Jim is a friend of mine.

And besides, it made me feel real smart to be able to manifest a quote out of thin air, as if I was saying *watch this* as I scratched the words down.

Then I collected on my end of the bargain and began to read her little questionnaires. I was shocked; they were right on:

> Gender: female; age: 24; occupation: sales;
> What is leadership? "Organizing people around
> a common goal."

> Gender: male; age: 26; occupation: programmer;
> What is leadership? "Standing up for what you
> believe in."

> Gender: female; age: 28; occupation: marketing;
> What is leadership? "Sticking your neck out
> when it's the right thing to do."

And on it went, just like that. Really good, thoughtful, and, in my opinion, accurate definitions. But then I found the one that said it all.

> Gender: male; age: 23; occupation: unemployed;
> What is leadership? "If I knew, I'd have a job."

"Now this is brilliant," I said. "'If I knew, I'd have a job.' He's right, I bet."

If even some unemployed slacker sitting on the beach knows how important leadership is, then I'm in the right business, I was thinking as I handed the pile of papers back to her.

"Can I play too?" He had been sitting next to me on the wall, listening to our conversation. "Sure," she said and handed him the clipboard.

"You write it down for me," he said. Salt-and-pepper hair stuck out from under his floppy black beach hat.

A newly sprouting goatee pinched up at the corners of his mouth as he smiled. "Four words that describe leadership," he counted them off on his fingers. "Love. Energy. Audacity. Proof."

She wrote on her clipboard. "That's it?" she asked. "Yup."

"Want to explain?" she queried, looking a bit befuddled. "Nah. Shouldn't need to. Except for one thing."

"Yes?"

"That's not just leadership; it's Extreme Leadership."

"Meaning?"

"Think about it for a while. You'll figure it out."

"Oooh...kay..." she said in that exasperated, drawn-out way that suggested eyes rolling behind her shades. She wandered off down the beach.

"That sounded pretty good to me," I said to the dude. *Dude* seemed to be the appropriate label. From his overall getup, the open Hawaiian shirt, Volcom flip-flops slung over his shoulder and baggy khaki shorts, he could have passed for late twenties. But the graying hair and wrinkles around his eyes suggested a few more years. It could have been too much sun. Or too much experience. I couldn't tell.

"It ought to," he said. "I heard you talking. You teach leadership, right?"

"I try to."

"There is no try. Only do," he croaked in a spot-on Yoda voice.

"Oooh...kay..." I said in that drawn-out way that suggested

eyes rolling behind my shades. I slid off the wall and stretched, trying to say "Gotta go!" with every bit of body language I could muster.

"Good to meet you..." he extended his hand.

"Steve," I said.

"Edge," he said.

"Come again?"

"Edge. Spelled E-D-G, with a soft g."

"Edg, as in *on the*?"

"Or *over the*."

"Okay, Edg, have a good one."

"Always."

Yup. *Dude* was the right label.

2.

Later that night, somewhere between sleeping and dreaming, I kept seeing that goateed face turned up in a smile and hearing his words, "love, energy, audacity, proof," like a persistent mantra. That and the girl's questionnaires got me thinking about my own leadership journey.

As a consultant, I had been a leadership evangelist for many years. I believed that effective leadership could help people to accomplish a couple of significant things at work. First, it would help create a culture so vibrant and healthy that when people woke up in the morning and thought about the imminent workday they wouldn't be overcome with a sense of dread and wouldn't doubt whether or not they could survive the day. Instead, they'd be filled with hope and the knowledge that they could bring themselves fully into their work and do something cool, something significant, something meaningful.

Second, an environment of total engagement would be more likely to create products and services so compelling as to virtually suck clients in the doors.

And even though I still felt as passionate as I ever had, I was beginning to suspect that, perhaps, I was being a touch idealistic. That scared me.

I know a lot of disillusioned consultants. When I was first starting out in my own practice, an older and supposedly wiser man named Patrick, who had built a sterling reputation as an executive coach and corporate change agent, told me that it was impossible to make a difference. No matter what you said or how you said it, no matter if you cajoled or threatened, no matter if you provided overwhelming evidence supporting your clients' need to change, they would never, ever listen to you.

"Then why don't you stop?" I had asked him.

"They pay me too much," was his response.

When the change agent becomes cynical, we're all in deep poop. I chose to dismiss Patrick as an over-the-hill burnout. So I started every project with hope and the conviction that the outcome would rock my client's world. And, with Patrick's sentiment echoing disturbingly in my brain, I ended each project somewhere between feeling mild satisfaction and what I can only describe as, *oh well, maybe next time.*

I was sure, though, that I'd had a positive influence on a good number of people. Right? They always paid me, didn't they? But if all I had done after all these years was broaden a few horizons and help a few folks try something a little different, had I really earned that money? Lying there at 3 a.m., I suspected I had not.

Then why don't I stop? My answer was different from Patrick's, because Patrick was a professional and I am a lunatic. Poet Charles Bukowski said it this way: "The difference between a madman and a professional is that a pro does as well as he can within what he has set out to do and a madman does exceptionally well at what he can't help doing."

I do this work because I can't help it; I have to do it. If that means I'm nuts, so be it.

That was, and I'm not being sarcastic here, a comforting thought that early morning. But love, energy, audacity, and proof? Was that what drove me? That sounded nice; they seemed like noble attributes, but they didn't seem like my attributes. I had to face it, the business of leadership was, for me, just that: a business.

Then it hit me, as the obvious sometimes does when I'm not paying attention, love, energy, audacity, and proof form the acronym LEAP. I'm not normally impressed by acronyms; I am, in fact, a bit leery of them. Many companies try to force fit unpopular, flavor-of-the-month programs into snappy, acronymic labels like QUALCRAP: quality circles, results, accountability, progress.

But the fact that LEAP was an acronym raised some interesting questions about Edg. Where did LEAP come from? Did Edg hear it somewhere or was it his own insight and creation? Was he talking from experience or just talking?

Alone in my room in peaceful predawn San Diego, I found myself curiouser and curiouser about the dude called Edg.

Curiosity killed the cat, the saying goes, and satisfaction brought him back.

Wednesday

3.

The next morning, I walked out to the boardwalk sipping a triple shot mocha and hoping that the caffeine would kick in quickly after my restless night. I walked down to the water, stuck my toes in, and watched the surfers zipping along the waves. They'd been out there since dawn, I was sure, just as they were every morning. They had the surf; I had caffeine.

"You surf?"

I jumped, splashing my morning fix into the sand. It was Edg, standing right behind me and leaning on his board, obviously delighted that he'd startled the foam out of me.

"No. I like to watch."

"Don't know what you're missing."

"Yes, I do. About three sips of precious fluids."

The water rushed in and cleaned up around my feet. "Sorry about that," he said, not meaning a word. "Let me make it up to you. You can buy us both another cup."

I followed him up the sand toward the boardwalk, thinking that at the very least, it could be fun to spend a little time with a fellow smart-ass. We walked up the stairs to Canes Rooftop

Grill. Edg leaned his surfboard against the wall and pulled a couple of stools up to the ledge overlooking the ocean.

As the waitress poured our coffee, I was plotting to satisfy my curiosity about Edg by digging around with inconspicuous small talk. I'd ask him where, if at all, he was working, where he lived, all the usual first conversation stuff. But I never got the chance.

"Watch that surfer," said Edg, pointing out over the water. I watched the guy paddle his board in toward the shore and stand up as the wave started to break. He rode for a very short time before falling ass-over-teakettle into the water as the wave crashed onto his head.

"Ouch!" I said.

"Wrong response, man. That's what the sport is about. What you just saw there was a victory."

"And the ocean won," I said.

"No. It's not that kind of victory. There's no winner and loser in this; it's not a zero-sum game. If you have to think of it that way, the surfer won some great experience that'll help him ride bigger waves later on. That's why every wipeout is a victory for the surfer. Same is true in your line of work."

"I feel a metaphor coming on," I said, finishing my coffee.

"Right. You got a problem with metaphors?"

"*Au A lot To do.* But spell it out for me."

"Surfing is an extreme sport because the wipeout is part of it. All extreme sports have that in common. And leadership, metaphorically speaking, is an extreme sport, too."

"You've got to be willing to take a risk. There's nothing new in that." I made a futile attempt to flag down our waitress.

"Very easy to say, but in business, especially, very hard to do. The irony is risk is a natural part of the human experience, and we accept it in many areas of our lives without realizing it. But a lot of businesspeople who call themselves leaders want things to be easy and painless. They're either kidding themselves or lying."

"Strong words."

"Look how people are dressed," he said, sweeping his hand over the boardwalk below. "Do you have kids?"

"Yeah."

"Do they wear baggy pants like those?"

"Oh, yeah."

"Do they skate?"

"A little."

"Skateboarders developed that style so they could wear knee-pads under their clothes. But most people who wear baggy clothes have never even touched a skateboard. They're called posers; they want you to think they're risk takers, and real skaters can't stand them. Posers try to grab the skaters' glory without putting themselves at risk. But wearing the pants doesn't make you a skater, wearing spandex doesn't make you a cyclist, looking at the world through Oakley shades doesn't make you a snowboarder, saying 'dude' doesn't make you a surfer and, in business, printing 'leader' on your calling card doesn't mean squat. People who wear 'leader' as a label without putting themselves wholeheartedly into the act of leading are just like fashion hounds; they're the posers of the business world."

The color was rising in Edg's already sun-reddened face. He still had a little half smile, but I could tell he didn't really find this funny at all.

"So they talk but don't walk," I said. "Kind of like the people that use all the new management buzzwords and leave it at that." That really got him going.

"It's a con job, is what it is," he said, his voice getting a little too loud for a public place. "These posers latch on to new jargon and catchphrases, but they don't do anything different. You ever been *empowered*, Steve? You ever *empower* anybody?"

"I suppose so, yeah. But that's hardly a new buzzword."

"No, it's not new, but let me show you what it typically looks like. Let's say you work for me." He pushed his stool back from the ledge and stood over me. "My boss recently came back from an off-site where they talked about empowerment, and she's got the religion now. So, the first thing she does back in the office is fire off an email to all of her direct reports, including me, saying that from now on we're going to *empower* people around here. So, now I'm going to *empower* you. What's my motivation here? Why am I going to do this?"

"Your boss told you to."

"Exactly. I damn well better or I may get And designs out of a job."

He began his little demonstration.

"What does empowerment mean to you, Steve?"

"Well, it's…"

"I'll tell you what it means. It means that from now on *you* are gonna start making decisions to take better care of our customers and improve our processes and all that garbage. Got it?"

"Yessir," I said, being the good little role-player.

He raised his arms and waggled his fingers over my head.

"Feel anything?"

"Yessir," I said, still playing along.

"You better," he said, waggling enthusiastically. "Steve, I empower you to go out there and make decisions to please the customer, yada, yada, yada. Now go forth and be thou empowered.

A little advice, however: *don't screw it up*. And before you make any decisions, check with me."

I chuckled as he received a round of applause from the folks at the next table.

"Okay, I get it," I said. "That's a poser talking."

"Exactly," he said, perching back on his barstool. "That's using a new buzzword with the same old garbage associated with it, behaviorally speaking. It's not empowerment."

We talked about all the buzzwords we'd heard over the years. It was like visiting the Management Jargon Hall of Fame, including such classics as MBO, MBWA, customer focus, quality circles, learning organization, value-add, thinking outside the box, excellence, downsizing, rightsizing, flattening, densepacking—don't ask me what *that* means—and reengineering to name, believe it or not, a few.

I remembered when Michael Hammer and James Champy's *Reengineering the Corporation* came out in paperback in May of 1994, how businesspeople stopped "changing" things and started "reengineering" them—move your stapler from the left side of your desk to the right side and *voilà!* you've reengineered your workspace. I had a friend going through a divorce at the time who told me he was "reengineering his domestic strategy." Very few people and organizations really understood the meaning and methodology that Hammer and Champy intended, and consequently didn't really reengineer anything, but they sure knew how to use the word in a sentence. This later led Champy to another conclusion: "If management doesn't change, reengineering will be stopped in its tracks."

Leadership, we agreed, was another one of those buzzwords. "Everybody calls himself or herself a leader nowadays," said Edg.

"We used to go to management training, and now we go to leadership training. We are team leaders, program leaders, project leaders, thought leaders, market leaders, and cheerleaders. We are political leaders, and we are community leaders. We lead our companies, we lead our families, and we lead our lives. We have diluted the meaning of leadership to such a profound degree that it's become just another label. But leadership is not that easy, so we con ourselves into believing that the word is the same as the action."

"'Con' is a bit hyperbolic, don't you think?"

"Isn't that what a con artist does?" he asked. "He'll promise a sure thing. He'll offer you ease and security without any possible chance of falling or failing. He'll guarantee what you want, when you want it. Then he'll take your life's savings, scoot off to the Caymans, and suck piña coladas squeezed from your hard-earned pineapples. We are our own worst con artists if we use safety and security in the same sentence as leadership.

"The ability to lead doesn't come from a snappy vocabulary, the books you've displayed on your shelves, your place on the organizational chart or that fashionable title on your business card. Leadership is always substantive and rarely fashionable. It is intensely personal and intrinsically scary, and it requires us to live the ideas we espouse, in irrefutable ways, every day of our lives, up to and beyond the point of fear."

"So, we're back to leadership as an extreme sport," I said, trying to pull a thread through the rant.

"Yeah. Extreme Leadership is what I'm talking about. Living in pursuit of the OSM."

4.

By this time, it was clear to me that Edg was no beach bum. At least not full time. He had obviously been around the corporate world in some capacity, and his conclusions were very similar to my own, which in and of itself didn't lend him any credibility. But I still didn't know a thing about him. Once again, I was going to ask him for his credentials, as it were, and I was going to ask how he'd come up with that LEAP idea, but he distracted me with another damn acronym.

"What, dare I ask, is an OSM?"

Edg called the waitress over and asked for more coffee and a pen. "First, you have to learn how to spell it." He grabbed a napkin and scribbled. "Like this: capital *O*, capital *S*, exclamation point, capital *M*. OS!M." He stirred his coffee with the pen.

"And that stands for...?"

"I'll give you an example. Then you tell me what it stands for."

"Okay," I agreed, without his asking me to. "You know what street luge is?"

"Like regular luge without the snow?"

"Close enough. Now, imagine that you're lying flat on your back on a long, wheeled sled, kinda like a skateboard, perched on the top of a steep hill. This isn't your serene, pastoral, snow-covered hill; it's an asphalt slope lined on both sides by parked cars. At the bottom of the hill, a quarter of a mile away, is a major intersection. And the traffic light down there is your finish line. Get the picture?

"Your friend pats you on the helmet, gives you a mighty thrust toward Main Street, and whoosh! You are gravity's love slave. The asphalt is blazing two inches under your back, parked cars are screaming past your head, and you can't stop, you can't turn back, and right there, in that moment, there are only two words on your mind. What are they?"

"Oh Shit!" I yelled, momentarily stopping the conversation around us.

"Exactamundo!" exclaimed Edg. "Now, picture this: You'd been preparing to give a presentation to the executive team of an important prospective client. You and your team had worked for days on the numbers, the graphics, and the perfect words. You had practiced in front of the mirror until it cracked, you had mumbled the entire spiel in your sleep for a week—so says your spouse—and now you're walking across plush gray carpet to the front of the boardroom. You reach the oak podium, turn, and look out at the grim audience of folded arms and Brooks Brothers suits, and you can't run away. Right there, in that moment, what are you thinking?"

"I want my mommy?"

"Try to stay with the theme here, Stevie."

"Okay. Oh Shit! Again."

"Right! OS!M. You've just had an Oh Shit! Moment, and it's the natural, built-in human indicator that you are doing, or are about to do, something truly significant and you are, rightfully, scared out of your gourd."

"And you're saying that's a good thing?"

"Absolutely. We've been conditioned to believe that fear is bad. And, yeah, fear can save your life or keep you from doing something stupid, but avoiding it can also keep you from doing something great, from learning something new, and from growing as a human being. Fear is a natural part of growth, and since growth, change, and evolution are all on the Extreme Leader's agenda, fear comes with the territory."

"So, the Extreme Leader pursues the OS!M."

"Yeah, but that's the easy part. Pursuing the OS!M, as I just described it, is a private, personal endeavor. But a leader lives under a microscope. I'm not saying it's fair or just, but people watch everything the leader does. Everything. They watch the body language and facial expressions, they listen to the tone of voice, they observe the decisions the leader makes, they listen to the leader's questions and how they're asked. Therefore, the most powerful tool a leader has is himself or herself."

"Leading by example. What does that have to do with the OS!M?"

"Simple. When you have your OS!Ms publicly, for everyone to see, you send a message that says we should all be doing this. This idea scares the hell out of most businesspeople. But I'll tell you, man, there are people in this world who love to screw up in public. It's their way of proving the power of their own convictions."

I was skeptical. While every business book I'd ever picked up talked about how important it was to encourage people to take risks and learn from their mistakes, I hadn't met many managers who relished the experience of falling on their own face. "Like who?" I asked.

"Like this rock climber from Adelaide, Australia. He was freestyling, that means no ropes and no harnesses, with a partner. He tried a new move, stretched just a little too far for his next handhold, and fell eleven meters off the mountain and landed in an olive tree. As he came to in the tree, he pulled an olive branch out of his side and realized that he was lucky to be alive. He looked up at his horrified climbing partner still clinging to the mountain and called out to him. Now ask yourself: if that were you impaled on that tree, what would you yell to your buddy?"

"Get help!" I said.

"Most people would. Here's what he said: 'Did you get that on film?'

"The only thing on that climber's mind in that near-death moment was the thrill he would get in sharing his muff with his mates. He wanted them to see that he was gutsy enough to attempt the audacious, even if he failed trying. That scar in his gut was his lesion of honor. That's not how most businesspeople operate, is it? Is that how you approach your work, Steve?"

"Meaning what?" I asked, wondering how I had suddenly become the subject of the conversation.

"Meaning this: You're leading an important project at work; you try something new, and it bombs. Miserably.

"You've skewered yourself in the olive tree. Do you yell, 'Hey! Everybody see how I screwed up there? Did we get that on film?' Probably not. The only reason you may want that film is to destroy the evidence, not to share it."

"I get the point, but I'm not so sure how comfortable I'd be having my failures immortalized."

"Comfortable!" he snorted. "Whoever said leadership is comfortable? You're missing the whole freakin' point: You screw up every day, and *everyone already knows it*. But when you show us that you can face your own screw-ups, when you can publicly acknowledge that you crashed and burned, when you can, metaphorically speaking, hoist your shirt in front of a hundred people to show us the scar that you earned when you fell off the mountain, we'll be closer to you as human beings. And we follow human beings; we don't follow idealized icons of unattainable perfection."

I knew he was right. And an image of me as a kid rushed

into my head: I devoured Superman comics by the pound and thumbed them until my fingers were inked up and my imagination was soaring. The Man of Steel was cool because of his superpowers: he had X-ray vision, he could fly, he could handle any adversary.

But ultimately, it was his imperfection that made him believable and compelling. He hid behind Clark Kent, his heart was torn between Lois and Lana, he grieved for his real parents and loved his foster ones, and he lived in constant fear of kryptonite. If the Invulnerable Man really were invulnerable, I'd have directed my loyalties to Disney comics.

Too many businesspeople, myself included, as Edg had pointed out, wanted to be invincible. They confused credibility with perfection and, therefore, would never dream of showing their scars and foibles to their employees. Asking them to have their OS!Ms in public would be like asking them to chew glass. I could think of one leader, though, who did pursue his own OS!Ms with the full participation of his team, and I shared the story with Edg.

5.

As a regional manager at a major brokerage firm, Michael had been working on his own leadership skills for several years. Despite his efforts, however, his retail branch region had consistently ranked last or second to last in his company's employee opinion survey. And in this rare company where surveys were taken seriously—the results were published and ranked—this was bad news for Michael's career. He was losing his credibility as a manager. Then he had an epiphany.

Even though the surveys specifically reflected the views of frontline branch employees whose lives were affected by their immediate supervisors, Michael assumed he was the problem, not the supervisors.

So he gathered his management team together, stood up in front of the conference room, and said: "I'm screwing up, and the numbers show it, so I want you to tell me what I'm doing wrong and what I need to do to improve." That was OS!M number one, I figured.

"I'm going to leave the room," he went on, "and I'd like you to get very specific and write down your ideas on flipchart paper. When I come back, we'll talk through each item."

And he walked out. OS!M number two.

A half hour later, he came back and knocked on the door. "We're not done yet," they said. Major OS!M.

Finally, after ninety minutes, they let him in. The walls were covered in flipchart paper with list after list of, what shall we call them, suggestions for his personal improvement as a human being. Monumental OS!M.

Michael knew that his reaction in that moment would make or break the whole exercise, as well as his personal credibility. So he took a radical approach and responded authentically.

"I'm really disappointed," he said, "in myself. I had no idea there'd be so much."

He didn't defend, justify, or make excuses. All he did was ask some questions to make sure he fully understood each item, and they talked together for the next couple of hours.

That night and the next couple of days, Michael told me, were the most difficult of his entire career. He was devastated and overwhelmed by the severity of the feedback and the immense challenge to follow through. He recovered from the initial shock, however, and the next round of surveys ranked Michael's organization second from the top in the entire company, with jumps of eighty to ninety percent in some measures. That's a leap no matter how you look at it. But the funny thing is, the improvement had relatively little to do with Michael's follow-up actions. It had everything to do with his team.

Without his asking them to, Michael's managers, inspired by the experience, went back to their branches and did the same thing with their folks. And for the first time, employees were personally engaged in the improvement of their own work environment.

By publicly seeking out those OS!Ms, Michael not only jump-started his organization, he also blasted his own career into orbit. As his reputation as a leader spread, he was promoted, with the near-unanimous recommendation of his direct reports, to take responsibility for the entire US branch office operations.

"Great example," said Edg. "Michael willingly scared the hell out of himself, because he knew that getting intensely personal feedback would be the only way to improve things. And that ultimately led to his and his team's success and to the heart of the matter: when necessary, the Extreme Leader will risk his or her own safety and security in order to grow the business and, just as importantly, develop as a human being.

"Safety isn't bad, but we often arrive at it by way of hazard and by learning from every break, scrape, and bruise. It often comes through the knowledge gained by having been unsafe. But the OS!M isn't about taking stupid risks, and it's not about putting yourself in harm's way for the hell of it or for some kind of gratuitous adrenaline rush. It's not about nauseating yourself or making yourself sick, though you may get sick in the process.

"You've heard of Jimmy Shea, the gold medalist for men's skeleton from the 2002 Winter Olympics?"

"Yeah. I saw him win it. That's some crazy stuff, those guys screaming down the track head first with their chins a few inches off the ground."

"Radical, huh?" he said with obvious delight. "An interviewer asked Shea if he could recall his first time doing skeleton, and he said, 'Oh, yeah. I felt like I'd just made the biggest mistake of my life. But when I got to the bottom, I couldn't wait to get back up and do it again.' No OS!M, no gold medal."

"So the OS!M in the right context is an indicator of growth," I summarized.

"Think of it like this: If the only reason you're avoiding taking on a challenge is because the idea scares you, then *that's the reason to take it on*. You have to pursue the OS!M, dude. That's how you know you're growing as a leader. And the bigger and more important the challenge, the more intense the OS!M."

"So the Extreme Leader takes on extreme challenges?" He glanced at his watch. "Tell me what you think of this. Carly Fiorina, as controversial as she was as the CEO of Hewlett-Packard, nailed it when she told an MIT graduating class that 'a leader's greatest obligation is to make possible an environment where people can aspire to change the world.' Is that extreme enough for you?"

I had also read Carly's speech—apparently Edg and I had some common source—but now I thought about it in terms of the OS!M. "Changing the world. Yeah, I'd say that qualifies."

"Let me put it bluntly," said Edg, as he stood and scooped

his surfboard under his arm. "If you're using all the buzzwords, reading all the latest books, and holding forth at every meeting on the latest management fads, but you're *not* experiencing that visceral churning in your gut, *not* scaring yourself every day, *not* feeling that Oh Shit! Moment like clockwork, then you're *not* doing anything significant, let alone changing the world. And you're *certainly not leading anyone else.* But you'll sure look snappy in your big, baggy pants."

He tapped a finger on the check, pointed at me, gave me a stiff salute, and turned to walk away. I waved good-bye to the back of his head and looked out over the ocean just as another surfer kissed the brine.

Thursday

6.

Intuition: it's the way a grandfather clock sounds at one second before midnight, or the way the phone sounds just before it rings. Phones don't actually ring anymore; they chirp, burble, vibrate; they chime a little tune like "Sailor's Hornpipe" or the theme to the *Muppet Show*. My kitchen phone burbled at the same moment as my oatmeal. I turned off the range and reached for the handset, with the gnawing feeling that this call would be important.

I had spent another restless night with Edg, not literally, you understand, thinking about our conversation at Canes, and it became blazingly clear to me that my life had been a series of leaps from one OS!M to another.

When I was seventeen, I graduated high school a semester early, moved from suburban Chicago to New York City—over my father's impassioned protests—and lived in a tenement apartment with my friend Sam and a couple of other free-spirited (meaning, unemployed) guys. Believe me, every day is jammed with OS!Ms when you're trying to survive on toast and Nestlé's Quik. But I grew up fast, and I wouldn't trade a nanosecond of my experience during that time.

By the time I was twenty-nine, I had lived in Israel for a year, started a folk/bluegrass band, terminated the folk/bluegrass band, started college, graduated college, started a rock band, gotten married, terminated the rock band, had three children, and started my own small brokerage firm.

My business had been a relentless struggle from day one: cash flow problems at work and at home, deception from people that I had viewed as trusted friends and advisors, and, finally, a partner who had bailed out on me at the worst possible moment. The last words I ever heard him say were, "I'm sending you a wire for twenty-five thousand dollars." The wire never came, I closed up shop, and he and I never spoke to or saw each other again. I wiped out, went down in a blaze of glory, crashed and burned—pick your metaphor—but I had learned how to, and more importantly, how not to, run a business. It turned out to be a great, invaluable, fabulous lesson that ultimately led me into my present career, but at the time, it didn't put oatmeal on the kiddies' breakfast table. Then I turned thirty.

That felt like a lifetime ago. And it felt like a minute. OS!M, OS!M, OS!M.

"Yellow!" I said into the phone.

"Steve?"

"That's me," I confirmed. "It's Janice."

"Janice! Man, oh man, I haven't talked to you in…"

"I think I'm about to get fired."

Janice had started out several years ago as my client and, during the course of a long consulting project, had become my friend. She was a dynamo who was accused of being a bit too aggressive at times except, of course, when she brought home the results. But she had a perpetual, infectious, and completely genuine smile that drew people to her, and an open heart that kept them there.

She was one of the few executives I'd met who really took personal development, hers and others', seriously. And believe me, I've met many executives over the years who gave up on their own leadership initiatives as soon as it became inconvenient or the organizational chart above them changed.

I remember a senior VP named Ron, a self-proclaimed cynic about *corporate change initiatives*, who experienced a sudden conversion to being a great champion of the company's new customer service training. One day he hated the whole damned thing and talked it down every chance he got; the next day he was standing on his soapbox in front of union employees and waxing eloquent on how marvelous this program was going to be.

A changed man? Hardly. The company had reorganized and Ron had suddenly found himself reporting to the program's sponsor.

"I took one look at the new org chart," said Ron, "and I realized how much I *love* this thing."

Janice was not like that. She had an internal sense of right and wrong and challenged herself to live up to it whether or not the environment around her supported it.

She had a center of gravity, while people like Ron tumbled through space, hoping to find orbit around someone else's point of view.

Now, apparently, she was in trouble. I wasn't surprised, though. Her company, a biotech firm called XinoniX, had recently brought in a new CEO, and the president had subsequently left under the pretense of early retirement. Rumors were flying about what had really happened, with some folks speculating that Teddy Garrison, president and founder, had locked horns with the new guy and decided to bail. Garrison had hired Janice and made her senior vice president of marketing and his *de facto* second-in-command. They had been together since the first day XinoniX opened its doors.

"I really wanted to make it work, even though Garrison was gone," said Janice. "He left a great legacy and culture here. We were doing some very cool things right at the forefront of genetic modeling, and everybody was jazzed. Before he left, Teddy handed me the torch. I mean, he *literally* handed me a tiki torch and told me that it was up to me to keep things going, to keep the place lively, fun, and fast. To keep it XinoniX, in other words."

"And?" I prompted.

"And he left. Just like that. That was a month ago, and nobody's heard from him. I don't have any idea where he is, and I feel like I've been left out here to dry up and blow away. I can't believe he would just walk away from us. XinoniX was Teddy's baby, and I don't think it's an exaggeration to say that every employee from top to bottom would have followed him anywhere. This was our baby, too."

"But you stayed."

"Yeah, I stayed. I put the torch in my office as a reminder and went to battle with the new guy."

"What's his story?" I asked, knowing that there had to be one.

"I think this sums it up: His nickname at his previous company was The 51% Guy."

I hadn't really been following the XinoniX story in the business press, so I hadn't heard the new CEO's name, but hearing that handle gave me chills. I told Janice that I knew The 51%

Guy; he had hired me several years ago at his company to "teach leadership to those people." He hadn't said it that way, exactly, but as it turned out, that was the gist of it. He was infamous among the employee ranks for two incidents that epitomized his management approach.

Once, at an all-hands meeting, he had stood up and said: "I want your input and opinions on things around here. I want to know what you think. Just remember, I have fifty-one percent of the vote." The employees had been so angry that they were still telling the story ten years later when I showed up. The fifty-one-percent rule, as it came to be known, meant, "Talk all you want, but this is my show. If you don't like it, go home." And judging by his nickname, it was his legacy. When I first heard that story from some employees in the company's distribution center, I wondered if he'd been misunderstood. Maybe, I had said to them, he was trying to say that he wanted their ideas, and that he'd use that valuable input in making his decisions, which, I added, is a very smart way to run a business. They laughed at me.

Around the same time of his little speech, apparently, a few of the employees were in his office offering their valuable insights into the improvement of the distribution center, and in the middle of the conversation, The 51% Guy picked up a glass of water from his desk and said: "You see the water level in this glass? Watch what happens when I stick my finger in there. See how the level doesn't change much if my finger is in the water or out? See that?" He wagged his moist index finger in front of their faces. "This is you," he said. "Whether you're here, *dunk*, or not, *wag*, makes no difference to us."

I knew this wasn't hard science, but when I put the

fifty-one-percent speech together with the finger-dipping anal-
ogy, I got pretty clear anecdotal evidence that The 51% Guy was
an autocrat at best, and more likely a dictator. The leadership
training that he'd sponsored was nothing more than a vain attempt to bolster his image. The 51% Guy, Bob Jeffers was his
name, was a poser.

"That's him," said Janice. "It was clear from the start that he's
the only one on his agenda."

"So you and Jeffers don't see eye to eye, I'm guessing."

"First he tolerated me, then he fought me on everything, and
now he's ignoring me. In other words..."

"You think you're about to get canned?"

"Yeah, if I don't quit first. And I need your help."

I was already thinking about companies I knew that would
snap Janice up in a heartbeat, but I was confused about why she
was coming to me. She knew everybody in the San Diego business community and had a great reputation in her field.

"I need to find Garrison."

"I don't understand," I said.

"What I mean is I want you to help me find him."

"Me? Who am I? Sam Spade?"

"Listen, Steve," she said. "I told him about the work you did
with me, and he said that he really wanted to meet you. I think
if you could find him, he'd talk to you."

"And then what?"

"You can talk him into coming back."

"So...you really want to stay at XinoniX?"

"Only if things change."

"Okay. I'll see what I can do, but only on one condition."

"I'm listening."

"You don't quit. And you and I start working on what you're going to do at XinoniX if Garrison's answer is no."

She hesitated on the no-quit clause and then said, "Deal."

So, I promised Janice that I'd call around. I did have a little time before my next trip, and, who knows, this could be kind of fun. *I'm going to need a new notebook,* I thought to myself in a voice vaguely reminiscent of Humphrey Bogart, *and a trench coat.*

"What makes Garrison so special?" I asked before I signed off.

"Well, there are a lot of specifics. He's smart, charming, a great visionary, and all that, but there's one thing about him that stands out above everything else."

"What's that?"

"He loved this place."

7.

Apparently, it had happened this way: Janice had gone to work that morning after our chat and conducted her traditional morning rounds of cubicle city. She always made a point of checking in with everyone on her staff before the chaos of the day came crashing down, and lately she'd been particularly vigilant. Her team had been busting its hump to finish its new marketing plan, and they were more exhausted than usual. The morning's informal face-to-face with their ostensibly fearless leader meant a great deal to the team, Janice knew, but it also gave her the emotional boost she needed to get through another day in the new XinoniX regime.

This day seemed to promise no more turbulence than usual.

That is, until she found the Post-it note on her computer screen. It said: "My office. Now. Jeffers."

She peeled the note off the screen and, with her blood pressure on the rise, headed off down the hall.

This, apparently, is how it happened: Her new boss invited Janice into his office and asked her to have a seat in the plush, leather banker's chair. He sat behind his desk, perched on his wingback, ergonomically designed Herman Miller marvel, several inches above Janice's line of sight. He held up the lime-green folder that contained Janice's team's marketing plan, ceremoniously waved it in front of his face, swiveled his chair efficiently to the right, and dumped the contents into the trash can.

And then, apparently, without a word, without a whisper, without so much as a grunt or a sigh, Robert J. Jeffers, The 51% Guy, got up and left Janice alone in his office.

8.

I was back at Canes enjoying an afternoon shot of espresso and thinking about my new role as the accidental sleuth. The connection, such as it was, with Janice, Jeffers, and me was too eerie to ignore. Synchronicity is what they call it, I think; I call it eerie. Still, I had no idea where to start looking for Garrison; I was having a hard enough time finding myself, let alone anyone else.

"Dude!" He had a way of sneaking up on me.

"Were you looking for me," I asked, "or is this just a happy coincidence?"

"I think it's called synchronicity," he said, sending a ripple up my spine. He was wearing a bright yellow Hawaiian shirt patterned with ripe, bulbous pineapples. I could see his eyes crinkling into a smile behind small, round sunglasses. He was, once again, the picture of beach hip.

"I've been thinking about you," said Edg as he parked himself at my table. "You and I have a lot to talk about, so I want you to meet me every day for the next four days."

"And I want *you* to dance the hula with a bone in your nose," I said.

"Really?" He seemed to be considering the possibility. "Why?"

"I guess I'm asking you the same question, Edg."

"At the risk of sounding mysterious," he said, "I'll just say that we'd be doing each other a great favor."

Well, that did sound mysterious and, frankly, a little bit wacky. I guess that's why I agreed. Besides, the truth was that I'd been thinking about him, too, and I had a few questions that lingered from the day before. I explained to him that I was working on a project for a friend and wasn't sure how much of my time that would chew up, so he'd have to be flexible with the schedule. "And what, exactly, is on the agenda for our daily meetings?" I asked.

"LEAP," said Edg.

And we did. Right into my car.

9.

"Where are we going?" I asked, feeling odd because I was the one driving.

"Go north, young man," said my passenger as he stuck his head, dog-like, out the side of my Mustang convertible.

We drove in silence up the coast toward North County, San Diego. We passed through Pacific Beach, La Jolla, and Del Mar, places known throughout the world for their beauty and wealth. Prime real estate with ocean views. You can get yourself a nice little pad for a few mil. I made a mental note to do that as soon as possible.

As we passed through Solana Beach, Edg directed me to turn right into a boulder-bordered driveway. I swung the Mustang eastward. The ocean view disappeared and, suddenly and shockingly, we were driving through a trailer park. A trailer park? Along the ocean? I didn't know which was stranger, the fact that it was here at all or that I'd never noticed it before.

"This where you live?" I asked.

He pointed ahead up the narrow, shrub-lined street. "Park there," he ordered, obviously ignoring my question.

"Ain't you the cryptic one," I said as I pulled the car over.

"Let's go!" He launched himself over the car door and ran up the pathway to a doublewide with a red rose bush planted on either side of the faux oak door and, without knocking, disappeared inside.

"Okay...I just need to turn the car off and close the top and stuff like that," I muttered to myself, "and I'll be right along. Go right ahead; don't wait for me..."

He'd left the trailer's door open, so I took that as an invitation and stepped over the threshold as fragrant rose-scented air filled my head.

I've always expected trailers to be dark and uninviting, but this one was filled with sunlight from a floor-to-ceiling bay window that looked out over a small, meticulous garden of bougainvillea, jasmine, and more red roses. Edg was standing out there with an older man, and they were just dropping their arms from what had obviously been a very warm embrace. They both looked my way and gestured for me to join them.

As I passed through the French doors, the man grasped my right hand firmly in his own and put his left hand on my elbow. His short, silver hair, glistening in the sunlight, was dramatically set off against his dark brown skin. He was a blend of African and Asian descent, I thought, and he reminded me of people I'd met in Trinidad several years before, who were some of the most exotically beautiful people I'd ever seen.

I know that it's a cliché to describe someone's eyes as twinkling or bright as if lit from within, but you'll have to excuse me because they were. And the relative darkness of his skin made his gray-blue sparklies even more noticeable as they locked onto me. His smile was full and warm and somehow familiar.

"Steve, meet Pops. Pops, Steve," said Edg.

"All my friends call me Pops," Pops reassured. "And I'd consider it an honor if you would, too."

He could have finished his sentence with, *this is CNN*, and I wouldn't have been surprised. His voice was as deep and resonant as James Earl Jones's.

We sat down at a small table under a jasmine-laced lattice, and Pops poured the three of us water with slices of lemon and orange floating on the top from a wide pitcher.

"I've told Pops all about you," Edg said with a bit of mischief in his voice, "and I think you already know a lot about him."

"Sorry, I don't..."

"William G. Maritime is what I'm called by the world at large," said Pops, also with a bit of mischief in his voice, "especially by the business press."

STEVE FARBER   53

I must have looked really brilliant with my mouth hanging open like that. William Maritime was a veritable business god. He was kind of a cross between a less flamboyant Richard Branson and a less explosive Ted Turner with a dash of Mother Teresa thrown in for depth. No wonder his smile was familiar, I'd seen it on the cover of *Forbes* and *Businessweek* as well as *People* and—I wasn't sure about this one—the *National Enquirer*. I seemed to remember a headline that said something like "Mystery Multimillionaire Maritime Marries Martian in Secret Ceremony." But I might have made that up.

What I did know was W. G. Maritime and Son was one big-ass company with a reputation for both bottom-line performance and community responsibility. It was one of those enlightened companies that management gurus were always talking about, and it was frequently cited as one of the top ten companies to work for in America. William Maritime's quotes were almost as ubiquitous as Jack Welch's. I myself had a PowerPoint slide saying,

> "Love the players or lose the game."
> —William Maritime
> *CEO, W.G. Maritime and Son*

I wasn't entirely sure what it meant.

He had started out in the boat-leasing business and over time had diversified, GE-like, into everything from entertainment to industrial steam-cleaning equipment. And then, one day a number of years ago, he retired and all but vanished from the public eye. That was a fact, but whether or not he retired to marry a Martian was, to my knowledge, never verified. What was irrefutable, though, was that the man was a legend, and the legend had just poured me a glass of water in a small garden behind his trailer home.

"I...," I said confidently, "I...am," I continued, building on my original proposition, "in the Twilight Zone, right?"

Edg howled, clearly delighted by watching me scramble for equilibrium. "No, it's the real world, dude. Trust me on that."

"Edg and I go back a ways," said William "Pops" Maritime, "and when he told me about your chance meeting and subsequent conversation, I asked him to bring you along on his next visit. So here we are. Good enough?"

"Sure," I said. "But we gotta make it snappy, because I'm expected for high tea at Buckingham Palace."

"Good sign," said Pops, grinning in the sharp sunlight. "The shock passes quickly."

10.

If you had told me this morning that by midday I'd be sipping citrus water with William Maritime, I'd have laughed in your face. But there, undeniably, I was, and I wasn't going to miss this opportunity to pick his very large, iconoclastic brain.

"Have you heard of the term 'OS!M'?" I asked, testing to see if he and Edg had ever had that conversation.

"I sure have," he said.

"What do you have to say on the subject?"

"The boy got your attention, didn't he?" said Pops, cocking his thumb toward Edg. "Well, it's a clever acronym, and it's memorable as a concept, and there's certainly no doubt that it's a legitimate and important aspect of the human experience in general and the leadership experience in particular." He paused and took a long, thoughtful sip of water. "But if you stop there, you miss the whole point of leadership."

"Which is what?" When that question leapt, reflexively, from my lips, I felt immediately childish. He must have meant that in a rhetorical way. Leadership is a multifaceted, complex subject; it can't have a whole point. I was being naïve to think that he was actually intending to complete the thought. But my question hung there in the air like a small but conspicuous cloud of cigarette smoke, too late to be sucked back in unnoticed.

He looked at me, expressionless.

"Never mind. Stupid question," I backpedaled. "There's no such thing."

"Let me ask you a 'stupid question,' Mr. Farber. Why do you care?"

"Well, assuming that there actually is a whole point of leadership, I care because I'm a student of the subject. I care because it's my job to help businesspeople to be better leaders, and I care because..." I heard my own voice trailing off and echoing down a long, empty cavern to nowhere.

"So the answer is 'because,'" he said.

"I know I can do better than that. You just caught me off guard."

He let me off the hook with a wide, warm grin. "I understand. Very few businesspeople take the time to reflect on why they care about anything they do: why they care about the decisions they make, why they care about their customers and employees, or why they care about their business beyond the paycheck. So don't feel bad. But that's one question that will never catch a true leader "off guard," as you say."

"But aren't you making a rather big assumption there?"

"Am I?"

"I think so. In order for business leaders to know *why* they care, you're assuming that they do. Care, that is."

"Of course."

"Are you telling me that managers, supervisors, and executives are always motivated by caring?"

"Of course not."

"I didn't think so."

"Leaders are."

"Actually," Edg jumped in, "care doesn't even touch it, does it, Pops?"

"No, it doesn't. I use the word *care* just to get us started. Care is a somewhat politically correct, watered-down version of the leader's true motivation. For an Extreme Leader, as Edg likes to say, it goes much, much deeper."

"So, Extreme Leaders are not motivated by caring?" I asked.

"Don't overcomplicate it, son. Of course they care, but their caring is rooted, ultimately, in love."

"Love." I repeated, with a splash of skepticism in my vocal tonic. I sat for a moment and let the idea sink in. "Love of what?"

"Exactly. Love of what. Love of what future we're trying to create together," Pops said, switching suddenly to the first person point of view. "Love of what principle we're trying to live out, love of what people I have around me, and love of what they want for their lives. Love of what customers I have, and love of what customers I might have in the future if I'm smarter, faster, and more creative in serving their needs. Love of what impact we can have on the lives of our customers and, if we're audacious enough, on the world as a whole. Love of what our business really is, and love for what, when we cut away the chaff, we really do at work every day."

He paused for a moment, as if to gather his thoughts, although they didn't seem to need any gathering. They were coming at me in laser-like, fully coherent force and concentration. Maybe the pause was for my benefit.

"If I love who we are, and if I love what we can be, then I'll love the process of how we get there. And in order to make it all happen, I will act boldly and courageously and I will, at times, fail magnificently. But my love demands that I try. *Demands* it."

"'A pro does as well as he can within what he has set out to do, and a madman does exceptionally well at what he can't help doing,'" I said.

"Bukowski!" Pops and Edg exclaimed simultaneously. "Jinx!" cried Edg, which had the charming and curious effect of cracking them both up.

"Bukowski, despite his drunken philandering," Pops continued, dabbing at his laughter-teared eyes, "got that one exactly right. It's the madness of love that I'm talking about. Or, at least it can look like madness to those who don't share the same passion.

"The title of that Bukowski poem is also apropos here: 'What Matters Most Is How Well You Walk through the Fire.' In the context of our conversation, having love and doing nothing about it isn't leadership by anyone's definition. You have to express it. You have to walk through the fire. And in trying to express my love in real, tangible, and meaningful ways, I will experience fear and I will face uncertainty. I will have OS!M after OS!M. That's the nature of leadership in the extreme: the dynamic interplay of love and fear. Acting out of love creates fear, and love gives me the courage to work through that fear."

"Love is the first part of Edg's leadership framework, too," I said, sounding like quite the organizational development weenie.

"Yeah. Edg's framework." Pops shot a smile at Edg. "You are one brilliant young man!"

I enjoyed the dynamics between the two of them, and I could feel that there was a rich history there. "I get the feeling that you've heard the LEAP thing somewhere before," I said.

"You could say that, yes. But love is not the first part of the framework; it's expressed *through* the framework. Here's the way I'd put it: *Love* generates *energy*, inspires *audacity*, and requires *proof*. LEAP, you see, is simply the Extreme Leader's active, dynamic expression of love."

"So it's *love* before you leap," I said. I received an enthusiastic cheer from my new friends.

"That's very good!" exclaimed the famous Mr. Maritime. "The Extreme Leader consciously and intentionally cultivates love in order to generate boundless energy and inspire courageous audacity. And he or she must provide the proof that it's all been worthwhile. Proof through the alignment between word and action, proof through the standing up for what's right, proof through measurable, tangible signs of progress, and proof through the experience of phenomenal success as well as glorious failure. That's the LEAP. And, if I can add to that, it's the LEAP that creates the OS!M. The OS!M is fear in the pursuit of creating something greater than the current reality. And the desire to create something greater is a bold expression of love. Simple as that."

Yeah. Simple as that.

11.

I had to admit that this love thing made a lot of sense to me. But, I also had to admit that the ghosts of a thousand executives seemed to be whispering, "Touchy-feeeeeely...touchy-feeeeeely," in my ear. I guess the haunting doubt showed on my face.

Edg jumped into the conversation, double-teaming me with his friend, Pops. "This goes directly to the bottom line. Love is just good business, dude. You know it from your own oh, let's call 'em *romantic adventures*."

"Come again," I said.

"Think back to your first date or two with that person you were really crazy about."

"You want me to think about a date?"

"Yeah. Stay with me for a minute. First of all, you really paid attention, didn't you? You listened intently to her every word, you noticed every detail: what she was wearing, what she ordered for dinner, and what songs she said she liked. And you took volumes of mental notes. You gathered data. And what did you do with that data?"

"I stalked her?"

"You responded; you acted. You delivered on her expressed desires and guessed at her unarticulated needs and responded to those, too."

"Were you there?"

"Not on your date, no. But I've been there myself. And so has anybody who has ever fallen in love."

I was beginning to think that maybe I wasn't so unique after all. What he said next confirmed it.

"So on the next date, you picked her up in that snappy Mustang of yours, but you left the top up because, even though you loved the feel of the wind whipping through the car, you remembered she told you how long it took her to get her hair just the way she liked it.

"At her door, you handed her one red rose, her favorite flower." He plucked one off a nearby bush for dramatic effect. "And, you escorted her on your arm to your waiting chariot."

"Am I that predictable?" He smirked. "So, what happened next, smart guy?"

"Then you headed for the opera house, because you knew she loved *La Traviata* and it happened to be in town, even though last week you thought *La Traviata* was an Italian restaurant and, frankly, still wished it were. Even though you'd rather see the Rolling Stones for the twentieth time, or get your teeth drilled by a very nervous dental student.

"But you also knew that your joy would come vicariously through hers. And your joy did indeed come when you saw those tenor-induced tears roll operatically down your sweetheart's cheek. Your joy came from the knowledge that you had done a very good thing and from the realization that you had won her heart."

Okay. So I had been to an opera or two over the years, and not because I'm a devotee of the genre. In fact, I don't think I'd ever chosen to go to anything where people said things like, "I'm a devotee of the genre," unless it was to please a loved one or impress an intended.

"Okay. You got me pegged, Edg. Guilty as charged. I'm a shameless, manipulative, conniving..."

"Hold on, Steve," Pops chimed in. "You're taking this the wrong way. This isn't about your dating rituals, this is about business."

"I'm not sure I'm tracking here," I said, feeling relieved that my love life had only been used metaphorically.

"Relationships in the world of business are won in analogous ways," Pops continued, "by paying nearly obsessive attention to the needs, desires, hopes, and aspirations of everyone who touches your business. By knowing not only when to stand firm on principle, there is such a thing as tough love, but also when to sacrifice some of your own short-term needs in order for us all to be successful in the long run. And by proving through your own actions that you really love your business, your customers, your colleagues, and your employees."

"You have to *prove* that you love the people at work?" My tone, I suspected, sounded a little more challenging than I had intended.

"This isn't some California, nutty granola, hoo-ha garbage," said Edg. "Saying that love has no appropriate place at work is like saying human beings have no appropriate place at work. It's nuts."

"I can feel the collective squirming of the entire human resources population," I said, hoping it would lighten things up. It didn't.

"Look," Edg continued, unabated, "you already bring your heart to work, and so does everybody else, right? It's not like you arrive at your office, pluck it out of your chest, and leave it throbbing on the sidewalk awaiting your return. So use it. If your heart is only performing an anatomical function, you are wasting one mighty fine organ."

"If you're not careful, you're going to miss the chance to let people know how much you care for them," said Pops. "The irony is that we often take for granted the very people that mean the most to us.

"It's like the story of the couple that had been married for thirty years. They're sitting around the breakfast table yet another morning, she with her coffee and he hidden behind his newspaper. She says to him, 'Honey, how come you never tell me that you love me anymore?' And he, from behind his newspaper, says, 'What do you mean? I told you I loved you when we got married. If anything changes, I'll let you know.'"

I chuckled, not only at the story but also at Pops's ability to tell it. He had great delivery.

"That's the way it is at work, too," Pops continued. "When someone does great work, you may give a pat on the back and say, 'Nice job.' But, if you don't take the time to stop, focus, and say how much you appreciate them, you end up wondering why they leave or run out of steam. So tell them now, right now, and don't wait another minute, because you never know when that next minute will be your last."

"So make sure to give timely recognition to the people you work with," I said. "With all due respect, Pops"—I was still having trouble calling him that—"that's the oldest management technique in the book."

He gave me a look that just about blew out the back of my head, and I got an immediate hit of the man's power. I suddenly realized, as if waking up from a daydream, that I had been lulled into thinking of this man as just a garden-loving, water-sipping, trailer-living, mellow and retiring Pops. But he wasn't. He was an empire builder. And, empires weren't built on a bunch of namby-pamby techniques.

He pushed his chair back and stood over me, never taking his eyes off mine.

"Once again, Mr. Farber," said W. G. Maritime, empire builder, "you have missed the point."

He turned away and disappeared into the trailer.

"What just happened there?" I asked Edg.

"He'll be back."

"Did I piss him off?"

"Just pushed a proverbial button, I think." He smiled and I felt better, though not much.

We sat and sipped our water in silence, and a few minutes later Pops stepped out into the garden carrying a pad of paper and a book whose title I couldn't quite make out.

"*Band of Brothers*," said Pops as he settled back into his chair. "I want to read you something." He put the pad on the table and then leafed through the book.

"This is a letter written by Sergeant Floyd Talbert to his boss, Major Dick Winters, in 1945. Talbert had been wounded on the front lines of the war with Germany and was confined to his hospital bed when he wrote, 'Dick, you are loved and will never be forgotten by any soldier that ever served under you or I should say with you because that is the way you led—I would follow you into hell.'

"Now, I want you to tell me, Steve," he locked his eyes on mine again, "does that sound like a *management technique*?"

"Well, no. But..."

"Let's be clear about this. When Talbert said, 'I would follow you into hell,' he was not speaking metaphorically. He had already followed Winters into hell. Literally. And he would do it again. And for only one reason: love. Love of his country, love of his brothers, and love of his major."

He stopped, and the silence rushed in around us. "Now, are you going to tell me that he was practicing a technique to get in good with his boss? That he was trying to kiss up, to manipulate the situation for his own future benefit? Is that what he was doing with this letter, Steve?"

"No."

"I have something for you," said Pops as he tore the top sheet from the notepad on the table.

It was a note to me from William Maritime written in a pointed, flowing script. Apparently, it's what he'd been doing when he went inside a little while ago. It said,

> *Dear Steve,*
>
> *You and I have only just met, and I can already tell what an extraordinary person you are. Before you deny it, let me assure you that I am known throughout the world as an astute judge of character. Here's what I know about you, Steve: If you will allow yourself to remember why you became a leadership consultant, if you will let your heart recall the ideals that it once held as inviolable truth, if you will strive to express them in your own unique Farber voice, and if you will permit yourself the glorious experience of helping others in their journeys, you will touch the world in ways that will surpass your wildest imagination.*
>
> *I, for one, would love to see it.*
>
> *Love, Pops*

What happened next was a total and unexpected shock: my eyes welled up and a single, perfect, crystalline tear rolled off my face and splashed onto the paper.

"Thank you," I said.

It was all I could get out.

12.

We were saying our farewells out on the curb next to my Mustang. Pops had walked us out, and he was now warmly grasping my hand and giving me one last little gem of wisdom. And dropping one last bombshell.

"Well met, my friend," he said. "I won't forget this afternoon, and I hope you won't either."

"Not likely," I said. The note was folded neatly and tucked into the back pocket of my jeans, where it would stay until I changed pants. And then it would move right along with me, I already knew, to the next pair. I would carry that note as long as the paper held out. I was already having thoughts of lamination.

"I suspect that we won't be seeing each other again, Mr. Farber." He saw the disappointment on my face, I'm sure. I'd been secretly hoping that I'd just earned a new mentor, and secretly doubting that I deserved it.

"This little trailer is just a way station, of sorts. It's been a nice place to lay low and collect myself before moving on."

"Moving on to where?" I asked, suspecting that I wouldn't get an answer.

"Remember, Steve," he said, proving me right, "the Extreme Leader cultivates love, generates energy, inspires audacity, and provides proof. You have to fall in love with your life's work again, my friend, or your energy will wane, your voice will falter, and there will be nothing to prove but the fact that you're taking up valuable space. And, you won't be helping to develop and perpetuate the Extreme Leadership that our fragile world so desperately needs right now.

"I challenge you to live up to this ideal:

Do what you love in the service of people
who love what you do."

"I like the sound of that," I said.

"There are three parts: *Do what you love*. Make sure that your heart's in your work, and that you're bringing yourself fully and gratefully into everything you do. If you're not connected to your own work, you can't expect to inspire others in theirs. *In the service of people* will keep you true, honest, and ethical, at the very least. If you're doing what you love, you'll make yourself happy. But Extreme Leadership is not only about you; it's about your impact on others. *Who love what you do* doesn't mean that you just find the people who love you and then serve them; it means it's your responsibility to give everyone you serve something to love about you and what you're doing. See the difference, Steve?"

"Yes," I said. "I do."

"And you, my son," he turned to an uncharacteristically quiet Edg, "I will see later, right?"

"Oh, yeah, Pops. I'm on you like white on rice, like spots on dice."

"Like cold on ice, but twice the price," chimed Pops. These guys had quite an act. I felt jealous, although I didn't need to.

"I love you, Pops," said Edg, and he gave him a hug and a tender kiss on the cheek.

Sensing my awkwardness at their unabashed display of affection, Pops turned to me.

"Okay. Hugs and kisses at work aren't always appropriate, I'll grant you that, but a son is allowed to kiss his father, isn't he?"

And then I got it: I had not only spent the afternoon with Pops and Edg, I'd spent it with W. G. Maritime and Son.

13.

When one returns from a parallel universe, he or she often discovers that time stood still back in the real world. Apparently, judging by the blinking light on my telephone, I hadn't been in another, timeless dimension at all. The world had just kept chugging along.

I ignored the message light, stepped through the sliding glass doors of my apartment, and drank in the view from my porch. The darkening water of Mission Bay was starting to dance in the oncoming twilight as a light breeze stirred the palms.

I had a unique relationship with that palm tree at the end of the walkway. It was a sentry, watching out for me from its vantage point eighty feet up in the sky.

One morning, about a year earlier, I had woken up in a blue funk. I was impatient with myself and with my career, and I was more than a little bit lonely. Recently divorced and relocated to San Diego, I was trying to find my new identity as a forty-something single guy coming to terms with the apparent unreliability of matters of the heart. I was weathering a difficult time in my life, and this San Diego morning, sunny and breezy to the rest of the world, was bleak and stormy on this side of my eyeballs. So, I set out on what I hoped would be a therapeutic stroll in the reliably salty sea air.

I headed down the path and turned the corner onto the walkway alongside the bay, passing directly through the shadow of my towering palm. I had heard a loud clattering and, a split second later, felt a sudden and forceful thwack on the top of my head. A young couple sitting near the water jumped up and looked over at me in surprise.

I had almost lost my footing but managed to stay upright,

even though I was a bit dizzy and disoriented. I looked down, and there by my feet on the sidewalk was a gigantic palm frond, its long, spindly fingers waving in the breeze in a mischievous gesture of greeting.

That son-of-a-bitch palm tree had staked me out. It had known my routine, waited for me to pass unwittingly into its target zone, and then with perfect marksman timing, from eighty feet up, it had let go one of its hands and smashed me on the head.

I had given a tentative wave to the couple to let them know that I was all right and offered an embarrassed laugh to acknowledge the absurdity of the scene that they had just witnessed.

Then I had looked up at the tree's remaining fronds, but they hadn't looked back and seemed, in fact, to look away suddenly so as not to be caught in the prank. "What? Is there a problem? I didn't do anything," is what I would have said had the roles been reversed.

Then I had noticed something truly odd. The day seemed brighter, and the breeze was invigorating; I felt good.

Sometimes it takes a smack from an old friend to snap you out of a deep funk. There was no law that said a new friend couldn't do that, too.

I was feeling like that again, standing there on my porch after spending several nearly surreal hours with Pops Maritime and Edg. Random meetings. Happenstance conversations. They all added up to one big, unexpected, exhilarating whack on the head.

The phone light was still blinking, and I paused for a moment to admire its persistence. It was time to renew my interest in the real world. The real world, however, didn't seem to be all that interested in me. One message.

It was Janice. "The 51% Guy has outdone himself. I'm *two seconds* away from walking out of this place. I made you a promise, though, and if you want to see me remain a woman of integrity, you'll get your butt to my office first thing in the morning." There was a slight pause. "Please?" her voice softened. She clicked off.

I felt an odd combination of flattery and annoyance as I listened to Janice's distress call. Flattered because she valued me enough to call me for help; annoyed because, frankly, I didn't feel like dealing with it right then. I was still trying to process all I had heard from my two new friends, and Janice's troubles were impinging on my reflective state of mind.

And then I noticed that I'd been unconsciously fingering a piece of paper in my back pocket. I pulled it out and read, "*You will touch the world in ways that will surpass your wildest imagination.*"

"Yeah, I'll be there." I said to the machine. "Wouldn't have it any other way."

Friday

14.

XinoniX headquarters were lodged in a growing cluster of biotech, Internet, and software companies in the Sorrento Valley area of San Diego. Many had hoped that this industrial neighborhood would turn out to be the epicenter of the coming biotech revolution. The recession had slowed things down a bit, but a lot of people remained hopeful. I was one of them, even though I had to admit that, as one who had struggled through physics and biology classes in school, the business of science was mystifying to me. But I didn't believe I had to understand something in order to be optimistic about its future. Sometimes intuition was enough.

I parked my valiant steed and walked through the automatic doors into the company's lobby. It's a tradition with this kind of company that no one shall pass the three-headed receptionist's guard station without an officially blessed and sanctioned security pass. Most of the passes say *escort required*, but they never live up to the promise in a way that would make it really interesting.

I signed the guest register and told the receptionist about my appointment with Janice. As I settled into the couch to await my liberation from corporate purgatory, I studied the XinoniX logo mounted prominently on the wall. The capital X on each end of the name was, I guessed, supposed to represent chromosomes. It made me think of Mexican beer.

XinoniX was also a palindrome—the same backwards as forwards. *Clever*, I was thinking, as Janice came through the security door. She was wearing designer jeans and a wool blazer over a simple off-white T-shirt. Casual, but confident: classic Janice. We gave each other a casual but confident hug and exchanged small talk as we walked down the hall past numerous pairs of curious eyes and ears.

We stepped into her office, and her demeanor shifted as she closed the door behind us. Something was off. She was crying.

She pulled herself together quickly, dabbing her eyes with a tissue that she plucked from a half-empty box on her desk. I kept quiet, not really out of respect, but because I had no idea what to say. Although Janice was a passionate and emotional person, teary displays were entirely out of character for her.

"Sorry," she said with resolve. "Have a seat, Steve."

"No need to apologize, Janice." I said as I lowered myself into an overstuffed chair. "Just tell me what's going on, and let's see if there's some way I can help."

"Okay, Doctor," she said wryly, her humor shooting through the gloom. She started pacing up and down in front of her desk as she caught me up on her latest encounter with Jeffers. She included every detail as though she'd rented the video and watched it several times. She wound up her account with a weary, "I've *had* it," and perched on the edge of her desk.

"Now what?" I asked. I get paid to ask the insightful questions.

"Now you help me figure out why I ought to stay."

I had no idea I was going to say it. It was as though a seed had been planted in my brain, and I didn't notice it until it launched this sprout from my mouth: "Why do you love this place, Janice?" I asked.

"Maybe you didn't hear what I just said. I don't love this place."

"Anymore."

"Right. Anymore."

"Then, why *did* you love this place?"

"The work we do is important."

"You're speaking in the present tense."

She stopped and considered the implication. "Yeah, it's still important."

"Why?"

"Because there's a great bunch of people here who have put in a lot of hours to make our products fly. They and their families have a lot at stake."

"That's true just about anywhere, isn't it?"

"Not like it is here. We develop software that scientists use to create new medicines."

"So?"

"What do you mean, *so*?"

"I mean there are a bunch of things a person of your talent can do. For someone of your caliber, a marketing plan's a marketing plan, once you learn the specifics of the business."

"This isn't just about marketing."

"No? What's it about, then?"

"It's about saving the world," she said without a hint of embarrassment.

I thought of my first conversation with Edg when he'd quoted Carly Fiorina: "A leader's greatest obligation is to make possible an environment where people can aspire to change the world." I assumed that Fiorina meant changing it for the better. Janice's agenda would qualify for that.

"So, you and your team are going to save the world. A bit lofty, isn't it?"

"Look," she said, pushing off from her desk, "Five hundred years from now, the time we're living in is going to be remembered for two things." Her face flushed as the volume in her voice went up a notch. "Number one, we developed the technology to destroy the human race. And number two, we developed the technology to save the human race." She was almost shouting now.

"And I want *us* to be remembered for the technology that saved the human race. *That's* why this work is important."

"Well, there you go," I said. "Want me to help you draft a resignation letter?"

"Very funny," said Janice.

15.

Love generates energy, but a few tacos also will do nicely in a pinch, I was thinking as I left the Jack in the Box and crossed Mission Boulevard.

I thought about my brief but powerful encounter with Janice earlier that day. She had forgotten why she loved her work and had just run out of steam. Once she remembered, her energy had come roaring back. It was an awesome thing to behold; right before my eyes she had summoned the juice to be an Extreme Leader at XinoniX, with or without the help of The 51% Guy.

After she threw the switch, so to speak, Janice had all but shoved me out of her office with an admonishment to "go find Teddy, like you promised." But not before she whispered "Thank you" with such gratefulness that I had felt wholly unworthy. I hadn't really done anything other than ask the right question at the right moment. And I hadn't even consciously known I was going to ask it.

Now, with my bag of tacos in hand, I was sauntering past the Mission Beach roller coaster and up to the boardwalk. The tourists and weekend beach bunnies had begun their migration, so the flow of pedestrian traffic was thick on this Friday afternoon.

I waited for an opening to traverse the busy walkway and finally found my opportunity in the short gap between a golden retriever pulling a skateboarder and a pack of three young ladies on Rollerblades. I dashed across the pavement, perched myself on the seawall, assumed the spectator position, and waited for Edg.

This was day two of my four-day commitment to him, and after yesterday's field trip to Pops's trailer, I was filled with anticipation. But I still had room for tacos.

As I munched taco number one, I thought about the mysterious Mr. Garrison. I hadn't yet done anything to try to locate the man, and I knew that Janice was hopeful that I'd be able to. While she and I were kindred spirits as far as hopefulness went, I didn't share her optimism in this instance.

After all, my sleuthing technique was severely limited. I had no clue how to proceed. I made a mental note to put in some kind of search time later that evening, which was my way of choosing to forget about it for the time being.

As I began to devour taco number two, I looked up the

walkway and noticed that the board-pulling golden retriever was headed back in my direction. People were jumping out of the way to let the dog bound through, laughing as she passed. With tongue flapping and ears whipping in the wind, the skater pooch was the belle of the boardwalk, but her passenger was also having a grand time, grinning broadly, waving to the crowd, and hamming it up as he zipped on by. No surprise there, it was Edg.

"Hey!" he said when he saw me saluting. "Hop on!"

I wedged the taco in my mouth, clutched the bag in one hand, and jumped down off the seawall. I jogged alongside for a moment, put my free hand on Edg's shoulder and hopped onto the board, expecting to be whisked away at blazing speed.

The dog was healthy, no doubt, but she wasn't Superdog. The sudden addition of two hundred pounds—all solid muscle, of course—to her load obviously exceeded her labor contract, and she went on strike. Immediately.

The dog slammed on her brakes, the board slammed into the dog, and Edg and I did an impromptu jazz dance over the dog and onto the pavement.

"You okay?" asked Edg.

"Mmmfifff," I said, as miraculously the taco was still lodged in my yap.

"Little OS!M there, dude?"

"More like an OF!M," I said as the dog tried to lick taco remnants from my face.

"The two of us were too much for Sadie, I guess," chuckled Edg as he pulled the retriever off of me.

Judging from her enthusiastic tongue wagging, Sadie, had she been a human, would have been chuckling, too. The saying, *happy as a clam*, applies to the entire golden retriever breed. It should be *happy as a pooch*, if you ask me.

I suggested that we take that happy pooch for a walk along the beach.

Edg handed his skateboard to an old guy with impressive dreadlocks who was sitting on the curb next to the lifeguard station. He said, "Thanks, Smitty," and motioned for me to follow him and Sadie down toward the water. Technically, this wasn't a dog beach, but no one, including the occasional member of the beach patrol, seemed to mind. Sadie, it appeared, had special privileges.

She pranced alongside of us and darted in and out of the surf, blissfully unaware that she was breaking the law.

We walked along in silence as I tried to sort out the questions about Edg that had been collecting in my head like so many bricks. They weren't stacking neatly. I was just about to launch into my interrogation when Edg motioned for me to keep quiet. He gestured toward Sadie.

"Watch her," he said.

As though on cue, the overgrown golden retriever took off up the beach kicking up little puffs of sand as she ran. She swung a wide arc to the left and headed straight into the ocean at full speed. She bounded over the first couple of small waves, and as the water deepened, she paddled furiously until a formidable mother of a wave crashed down over her body.

I gasped reflexively as Edg laughed. Sadie's head popped up out of the surf, and she propelled herself back toward the shore with professional ease. It was as close to body surfing as a dog could come, I figured. She sprinted out of the water and shook herself vigorously, sending a spray of fine mist in every direction.

Don't let anyone tell you that dogs don't smile. She was grinning like a child, no doubt about it, as she trotted back to us.

"Does she ever stop?" I asked.

"Not out here she doesn't. She loves the beach. And when Sadie's in love, Sadie's unstoppable."

"Wait, don't tell me," I said.

Edg's right eyebrow arched slightly as he looked at me. "Don't tell you what?"

"Love generates energy, right?"

"Guess I didn't have to tell you. To put it simply, the more love you have, the more energetic you are," Edg said, his words punctuated by Sadie's enthusiastic and expectant panting. "Without it, you're a drone."

He threw a stick of driftwood into the ocean, and Sadie took off after it like a shot. A few minutes later she was back, dripping with seawater. She dropped the stick at Edg's feet and looked up into his eyes.

"What do you think will happen if I throw the stick again?"

Sadie wiggled and danced around us, answering the question in doggie body language.

"I'll go out on a limb and guess that she'll fetch it." He threw. She fetched. And here she was again, a big, wet, furry déjà vu.

"How long do you think she'll keep doing it?" he asked as he let the stick fly. "Forever," he said, answering his own question. He was looking out over the ocean as he tossed and talked. He stopped suddenly and turned to look at me.

"You know why she'll keep coming back?" he asked.

"Why?"

"Because she's a dog."

He paused to let the profundity sink in. It didn't.

"And?" I asked.

"Kinky Friedman said, 'Money can buy the dog, but only love can make it wag its tail.' A stick is motivation enough for Sadie because, to her, there are few activities she loves more than the fetch game."

"And?" I repeated.

"Look," he said, "I know it's simplistic, but the point is people are not dogs; we're not content to spend our lives chasing sticks. We're far more complex than that, yet so many businesspeople throw sticks and expect others to fetch and come back again and again like good little doggies."

"I think it's safe to say that you've completely lost me."

"At work, if you want talented people to keep coming back, what do you do? Besides pay them, of course."

"You mean how do you energize and inspire the masses?" He nodded, so I answered my own question. "Most people will give a series of fist-pumping speeches, write rousing memos, print T-shirts, that kind of stuff."

"Right," said Edg. "But you're still missing the biggie."

"You mean the vision thing?"

"Bingo!" He chucked the stick, and Sadie bolted there and back again. "It's become conventional wisdom that in order to get people excited about the present, you talk about the future. You have a vision statement. Problem is, most vision statements are way too incomplete at best, and cynicism-inducing claptrap at worst."

"Agreed," I agreed.

He chucked the stick again. "It's easy to pump people up, but it's usually a temporary phenomenon. Michael Cunningham, the novelist, said, 'If you shout loud enough for long enough, a crowd will gather to see what all the noise is about. It's the nature of crowds. They don't stay long, unless you give them reason.'"

"Well said," I said.

"Leaders ostensibly use vision statements to give people reason, right?" Once more, he chucked the stick.

"And you're saying they don't?" I asked, feigning shock.

"Not hardly." He waited for Sadie to return, and when she did he told her to sit and then scratched her aggressively behind the ears.

"First of all, every business book you pick up will tell you that you need to have a vision statement, so any company that's done its required reading will have one. It develops like this: A group of senior executives, now known as the executive team, goes away on an off-site, sits down together and has a poetry contest. They try to hammer out just the right words and phrases, and they argue for hours— days, sometimes—over the choice of words. 'Should we call them *customers* or *clients*, are they *shareholders* or *stakeholders*, do we have *employees* or are they *associates*?' They tear their hair out, and they threaten, and they fight, and ultimately, at the end of the day, they have created a magnificent document, and they're so, so proud. So what do they do?"

"Get drunk?"

"They laminate it. Laminate it on little wallet-sized cards and hand out a copy to everybody in the organization. Then they hang a full-color calligraphy version in the reception area and wait for something to happen. After a time, they look around the company and are absolutely incredulous that nothing has changed. 'What the hell is wrong with these people?' they exclaim. 'Can't they read?'

"It's as if they expect the laminated card to work like a nicotine patch. Carry it close to your skin and the energy will somehow get into your bloodstream. It doesn't happen that way. Most corporate vision statements are generic and meaningless to the very people they are supposed to inspire. And they don't, to say the least, generate energy of any kind.

"They may as well say, 'Blah, blah, blah, blah, *company*. Blah, blah, blah, blah, *customers*. Blah, blah, blah, blah, *shareholders*. Blah, blah, blah, blah, *employees*.'" He threw the stick, and there went Sadie.

"It's simply a case of mistaken cause and effect," Edg continued. "A vision statement doesn't generate energy, love does, great ideas do, principles and values do. A vision statement that comes from a workshop exercise is usually about as energizing and memorable as a saltine cracker."

I'd witnessed that scenario over and over. One senior team of executives at a bank I had worked with did *The Vision Off-site* and came away with their very own snappy acronym: STAR. I can't remember what it stood for; I think it was service, teamwork, accountability, and respect. Or maybe it was synergy, tenacity, ability, and returns. What I do remember is that their frontline folks kept telling me they were confused about the organization's vision.

So, I went back to the executive team and I said, "Listen, I've got some feedback for you. Your employees are telling me they don't understand the vision of the company." That infuriated one of the senior executives, whose face turned so red that I thought his head was going to pop right off.

"What do you mean they don't understand the vision?" he had howled. "We did that! It's STAR!"

"Well," I had said gently, "the very fact that you are saying we did that means that you are *not doing* that. Maybe your folks need a little more than an acronym."

"Like what?" he had demanded.

"How about an anagram?" I had suggested. He hadn't appreciated my wry humor as much as I had, even though RATS was, I had pointed out, a great anagram for STAR.

"But vision from the heart is, by definition, an expression of love," Edg was saying. "And not only is that more energizing, it is energy. It's juice, man." He looked out over the ocean as Sadie bolted, once again, into the surf.

"Martin Luther King's 'I have a dream' speech was juice for a generation. He didn't have to hand out 250,000 laminated cards at the Lincoln Memorial on that hot August day in 1963. Watch the tape, it was pure energy. Juice. Life itself." He called to Sadie, and we turned around and headed back toward the lifeguard station.

He looked down at the sand as we walked. "Think about your clients, Steve. I'll bet the vast majority of them grossly underestimate the power of their own hearts. They have no freakin' idea how much energy they can unleash in themselves and those around them if they just put down that bureaucratic, banal, generic crapola and tell people why they love their businesses, and communicate their authentic hopes and aspirations for the future of their companies. Am I right?"

I flashed back to the scene in Janice's office. "I suspect so," I said. "So what's the remedy for the 'blah, blah, blah' corporate vision statements?"

"Burn the damned things," said Edg.

"Isn't that a bit harsh?" I asked. "What's next? Flags and bras?"

He let out a deep breath. "*Love generates energy* is our premise, right?" He drew a heart in the sand with the toe of his sandal. I remembered when my daughter was six, and we were visiting San Diego from our home in the landlocked Iowa countryside. On the beach one day, she'd surrounded herself with hearts that she'd traced in the wet sand. I still had a picture of it nearly twenty years later. She had been sitting, I realized with a sudden electric jolt, on the very same beach where Edg and I now stood. I shook myself and tried to concentrate on the present. Edg drew a second heart, then a third and a fourth, and he kept going until we were standing in the middle of a circle of hearts.

"The Extreme Leader's job," said Edg, "is to connect all those hearts, true?"

"Ideally," I said.

"No. Not ideally. Absolutely. Without that heart connection, you may have an employer/employee thing going on or a bureaucratic boss/subordinate relationship. People who don't have that heart connection won't try to change the world together. And if you're not trying to change the world, you haven't entered the realm of the Extreme Leader.

"And that, then, begs the question of how to establish the connection."

"So how do you establish the connection?" I asked, since he'd begged.

"By revealing yourself as a human being to those you hope to lead. So instead of reciting a vision statement, feel the intent of that statement, reflect on the ideals that it represents and take it all into your own heart. Then at every opportunity, whether you're talking one-on-one or standing in front of a crowd, you say, in essence, 'This is who I am, this is what I believe, this is what I think we can do together if we put our hearts into it. Look at how magnificent our future can be. Please join me and let's help each other make this happen.' Then you can burn the document because, in effect, you've *become* the vision."

"That's rare," I said. "I'm not really sure I've seen anyone do that in business."

"I've seen it," said Edg. "And the connection is electric."

"Energy," I said.

"Generated straight from the heart."

16.

Smitty was still on his perch watching the boardwalk traffic from behind his large, yellow-tinted glasses. Sadie ran up to him and pushed her snout under his hand.

"Sadie, Sadie, beautiful lady! How's my girl?" said Smitty, as he lowered his head and turned it to give the dog access to his ear, which she licked enthusiastically. "Did you enjoy your jaunt with Uncle Edg?" Sadie said, *Oh, yes, I sure did*, but not in those words.

"Steve, Smitty. Smitty, Steve," said Edg as he took back his skateboard from his dreadlocked pal. "Why don't you guys get acquainted? I'll be back in a flash."

Before I could protest, Edg was pushing away on his board.

"Have a seat, man." Smitty patted the curb. His dreadlocks fell around a face that sprouted the most impressive beard I'd ever seen up close. It was a ZZ Top sort of thing, but red and not as tame. His hair was so outrageous, in fact, that I found myself wondering if it was real. Smitty's head was a hirsute funhouse.

"He may be a while or he may not be back at all. One can never tell with Mr. E." His voice was raspy, and he spoke with a watered-down Texas drawl, evidence that he had once had an accent as thick as barbecue sauce.

"Sadie's your dog?" I asked, as I lowered myself to the curb.

"Not really sure who belongs to who," said Smitty. "She's a beauty."

"She knows it; that's for damn sure. She gets a lot of attention on account of it, too." Sadie wagged her body. "But she's happy to share some of that with me. Ain't ya, pooch?" Almost on cue, a flock of young ladies stopped on the boardwalk in front of us to fawn and coo over the dog.

Smitty offered a couple of hi theres and howdys, and the girls were polite enough to vaguely acknowledge his existence. He sat grinning through his beard like the sun shining through a hedge.

"Ah, yes," he sighed as he watched the flock flutter away. "Life is full of wonderful little exclamation points, ain't it?"

I assumed that the question was rhetorical.

"Ain't it?" he repeated, annihilating my rhetorical question theory.

"Yeah. Okay, I never quite thought of it that way, I guess."

"Yep. It's true. Exclamation points, question marks, asterisks... everywhere you look." He scanned the boardwalk through his yellow lenses.

Curiouser and curiouser, I thought, ignoring Smitty's blabbering. There was no sign of Edg; he had all but dumped me and taken off with no explanation, request, or instruction.

"So...Smitty," I said. "How do you know Edg?"

"Edg, Edg, Edg, how do I know Edg?" He grinned. "Well, I used to work with him, that's how."

My heart jumped a bit. I was about to hear an actual detail, a bona fide fact about Edg's past. "Doing what?" I asked, probably sounding too eager.

"Oh…this and that, I guess. When there was stuff that needed doing, I did it."

"Yeah, but what kind of stuff?" I was rapidly losing patience.

He paused for a split second. Then he said, "Oh, hell. It really don't matter. It was just a bunch of technical titty twistin', really. Point is, he made me a very rich man."

That was quite a punch line. I tried not to look surprised, which was about as easy as trying not to look like I obeyed the laws of gravity.

"And that is what allowed me to get started in my new line of work," Smitty continued, as though he'd said something as banal as "I scratch myself."

"Which is what?" I asked.

"I'm in the sign business." It sounded like, *sahn*.

"You make signs?" I asked.

"Nope."

"Then, what?"

"I read them.

"I'll show you what I mean," Smitty said, apparently in response to the way my face had scrunched up into one of his environmental question marks.

He got up and started walking with Sadie along the boardwalk toward the surf-and-skate shop on the corner across from Canes.

"Look there." He pointed, stretching out his tanned, sinewy arm.

The cement lamppost was plastered with papers and graffiti.

A bold bumper sticker reading, *No Fear*, was posted just above a flyer for a speed metal band called *Satan's Bastard Goat Child*.

"Good words of encouragement on that sticker, don't ya think?" he said.

"Excellent," I acknowledged. "Especially if you're going to that concert."

"How about this?" He put his arm around another pole that supported a sign that said *Unattended vehicles will be towed at the owner's expense*. "It's a fact of life just as sure as shit, right?"

"Meaning?" I asked.

"A lot of folks out there," he spread his arms to indicate the beach crowd, "are unattended vehicles. Four wheels, a chassis, and no driver. Nobody there to put the top up in a rainstorm. No sense, in other words, of *who* they are. Just tooling along and hoping someone will jump in and put 'em in gear before they get towed to the auto pound."

"That's a rather grim view of humanity," I said to Smitty the Sign Reader.

"Ah, c'mon. It's not grim or jolly. It's just the way it is, unattended vehicles will be towed. So...*attend*. That's just good advice, ain't it, Sadie?"

"Curb your dog," I said, quoting the famous sign.

"Now you're gettin' it! Great advice! It's all around us.

"We're surrounded by lessons; we just need to notice the signs and ask the right questions. Ask the right questions and you learn some pretty good stuff about what's goin' on around you. And when you realize that there's deep significance in seemingly insignificant things, the whole world pops to life, and everything becomes part of a 24/7/365 multidimensional, hyper-accelerated, interactive learning laboratory."

"Really." It sounded like a statement, but I meant it as a question. "What about that sign?"

"*No parking*," read Smitty. "That's pretty obvious, ain't it?"

"Or that T-shirt?"

"*Skate or die*," He recited. "Just another version of *No parking*, don't ya think? Keep moving; don't stand still. Life is movement; stagnation is death. No parking, skate or die." I felt a slight chill.

"So you're saying that there are messages everywhere?" I asked.

"Not really. Truth be told, all the messages are in one place... right here." He tapped himself on the head. "It's all in the interpretation, right? To most people, *yield* is only a traffic sign, but to me, it's a lesson about going with the flow, get it? Same sign, different meaning. The sign's just a stimulant. The difference is what I see in the sign, how I read it. The difference is right here in my itty-bitty brain. The sign just gets me to payin' attention."

"So, read signs and interpret their meaning," I mused.

"Yep. Read the sign, ask yourself what the lesson is, and you'll get you some wisdom at every turn. Let me show you one of my all-time favorites." He said it like *fay-vo-rites*.

Sadie and I followed Smitty up the boardwalk. He moved with surprising speed, cutting back and forth through the crowd. I had to trot to keep up, but Sadie never broke a sweat. Dogs never do.

About a half mile up the walk was a beachside strip mall with several shops, restaurants, a few offices, and a public restroom. I followed Smitty through a door that said *Men*, while Sadie, apparently a good sign reader herself, waited for us outside. Smitty opened a stall, and I headed for the other apparatus mounted on the wall.

"Wait," he said. "I want to show you something."

"Excuse me?"

"Nooo, no, no!" he laughed, picking up on my suspicious tone. "I want to show you the quintessential, classic management sign."

"In that stall?"

"In this and untold others."

I walked over slowly, pulling the sunglasses off my face so my eyes could adjust to the restroom's dim light. I poked my head inside the stall.

"There it is," said Smitty.

Expecting to see the graffiti equivalent to *mybosssucks.com*, I scanned the stall walls for anything of organizational significance. Other than a few phone numbers and testimonials to someone's ability to impart on me a good time, I saw nothing of note.

"You're looking in the wrong place—it's not graffiti," he said.

And then I saw it. And it wasn't the first time I'd seen it, either. It was just the first time I'd paid attention. Screwed to the wall over the toilet was a seat-cover dispenser with a notice that read:

Provided by the Management for Your Protection

"That, m'friend," Smitty said, "is the single most dangerous management myth of all time."

"Really," I said, once again making a question sound like a statement.

"Yup. First off, it's a lie: you will never, never see one of them ol' management boys wrapped in a tool belt and screwing seat-cover dispensers into the stall wall.

It's a facilities staffer that's covering your butt, not the management. In fact, the custodians of this building provide for the *management's* protection, not the other way around."

"So you're saying that it's not literally true."

"Yeah, sure, I'm sayin' that. But it's the attitude that really puts a barb in my bony backside."

"The sign has an attitude?"

"Yeah, man. It's arrogant. It's overinflated, self-indulgent, and pitifully self-important. Management, the benevolent protector. Management, the bestower of blessings. Management, the big mommy/daddy. What a load…pun intended.

"All you gotta do is read the business alphabet from Andersen to Xerox to see that it's a lie. In business, nobody provides for your protection. Except you."

"What do they call you, Smitty the Cynic?"

I followed him out of the stall, out of the men's room, and back out into the sunshine.

"I am not a cynic. Not by a Texas long shot. I'm just callin' it like I see it." He whistled for Sadie.

"You're saying it's not management's job to protect its employees. Your friend Edg, though, says that love is at the foundation of good business. So you guys disagree?"

"We're in picture-perfect agreement, as a matter a fact. There are different kinds of love, m'friend. A business should be socially responsible and ethically minded and all that good stuff. That's a kind of love, ain't it? And it should love its employees for devoting talent, time, and energy to the biz, and it should show it. But a business also has a responsibility to itself; it's gotta stay healthy. And sometimes that means makin' decisions and doin' things that'll piss some of its employees off. So don't it follow that all of us, as individuals, have to take responsibility for ourselves? We can't abdicate our personal responsibility to some supposed higher authority.

"Look around you, man. Forget the accounting scandals for a minute; do you see any *legitimate* companies that'll give you a job for life? Nope. Ever see anyone with piles of talent who lost a job? Yup. Happens every day, no matter what condition the economy's in. Sometimes love for the health of the company and love for individual employees smack right up against each other. Sometimes love hurts, and sometimes it's got nothing to do with personal love at all."

"Well, the world's changing, the market's changing, and some of those things are just unavoidable," I said. "They're beyond any one human's control."

"That's all I'm sayin', friend," agreed Smitty. "Nobody, not your friend, not your minister, not your rabbi, not your mullah, not your momma, and certainly not your management, is going to protect you from the big, wild world. And you know why?"

"I'm pretty sure."

"Because they can't. What they can do, what they should do, what they damn well better do, if they have an ounce of gray matter, is create an environment where people can thrive as adults and grow as leaders."

"Where people can aspire to change the world," I offered.
"Yessir! And, if and when you leave the company, you are more capable and experienced than the day you started. This ain't about protecting you from the world; it's about giving you the chance and means to change it.

"So, two things gotta happen, the way I see it. First, management has to stop pretending that they want to be your momma.

They can start by taking down all them bathroom signs, and then we'd put up ones that say something like:

> These covers are provided to you by a member of the facilities crew who works all day in a thankless job. Management doesn't even know how these got here, but we're sure they'd approve, because we all sit here eventually. With these seat covers, you have an opportunity to protect yourself. We recommend that you take it. After all, it's your ass."

I stared at him. "What a great metaphor," I said.

"But that's only the first part," he continued, ignoring my compliment. "Yeah, management has to stop pretending to be the great protector, but the rest of us have to stop askin' and expectin' them to be. We gotta get over the whole idea of *them*, as a matter of fact. We need to hold ourselves accountable and stop looking to blame them when things go wrong."

I knew he was right, of course. In every seminar I had ever taught, in every company and at every level, the subject of *them* always emerged, but I asked for an example anyway.

"Example? Well, it's universal. Sure as the sun will rise in the east, folks will end up blaming their woes on *them*. Managers blame their woes on *them*, the employees, and employees gripe about *them*, the management. Presidents and CEOs whine about *them*, the board, or *them*, the analysts, and we all moan about *them*, the shareholders. The conversation goes round and round like a Ferris wheel, and pretty soon you're not sure who's talking about who.

"Look, man, say that you're the management."

"Okay," I complied.

"And say, for example, you've just distributed another employee opinion survey. You ask *them* for their candid views on the company, but seventy percent of *them* don't respond. So you complain about how unresponsive *they* are, and then you ignore the feedback of the other thirty percent. With me so far?"

"Seen it a thousand times," I said.

"*They*, consequently, start talking about *you* or *them* as you're known to *them*, and how *you*, or *they* as you are known to *them*, don't really care about what *we*, or *they*, as they're known to *you*, have to say about *them*, or *you* as you're known to yourself. Still with me?"

"Here comes lunch."

"And where does it all end up? What's the big conclusion? 'They will never change,' they say about them."

"The classic organizational stalemate," I said.

"And it's all an illusion."

"Meaning?"

"There ain't no *they*."

"There ain't?"

"Nope. There's just *us*." He whistled for Sadie again. "She headed home, I guess."

"Not counting on you to provide for her protection, I take it."

"Even the dog gets it," said Smitty.

It was late and I was hungry, and after he declined my invitation to a steak dinner, Smitty and I said our good-byes. He walked south toward the lifeguard station where we'd met, and I headed north and away from this very unusual character.

With a vague rumbling in my stomach and a wisp of a smile on my face, I walked up Mission Boulevard toward the restaurant.

I had a lot to think about from my brief and bizarre conversation with Smitty: them versus us, protection versus self-reliance, blame versus accountability. At times, I admitted to myself, I did hope that someone would protect me. That someone would take a deep, personal interest in my well-being. That someone would lead me in my life. It just sounded so much easier than the alternative, which, I realized, was being a leader myself.

I looked up and saw a sign posted outside a small retail shop. *No loitering*, it read.

"Hmm," I mused. "Wonder what that means."

17.

All signs pointed to the fact that I deserved a big steak. That's why I soon found myself sitting in a small booth at Saska's Steakhouse, a Mission Beach landmark since God created cows. I looked around the small, dark dining room as I chewed on a tender piece of something that had once chewed its cud. The Christmas lights, a year-round fixture at Saska's, sparkled from beam to beam. My gaze traced a pathway starting at a brass-framed mirror, moved down the glittered wall to an indiscernible velvet painting, jumped over a couple of booths, and landed, finally, on the small, flickering candle flame cupped in a red jar in the middle of my table. I suddenly remembered what I needed to do. As I borrowed the White Pages from the bartender, I explained that it was dinner reading.

The brilliant detectives always start with the obvious, which is exactly why I had overlooked it. Why not see whether the elusive Mr. Garrison was listed?

He was. Hidden cleverly in the *G* section.

I fired up my cell phone and dialed the number. The phone rang twice, and I hung up, realizing that I'd given no thought to what I'd say when he—or worse yet, his voice mail—answered. Better to think it through first.

I collected my thoughts into a relatively coherent form and dialed the number again. A woman's voice said: "You've reached the number of Teddy Garrison. You may think that this is an answering machine. It is not. This is a questioning machine. And there are two questions: Who are you? and What do you want? And lest you think those are trivial questions, consider that most people go through their entire lives without ever answering either one." Beeeep.

The recording threw me. I'd heard that message before from my friend, Terry Pearce, who'd written about it in his book, *Leading Out Loud*. Whether Garrison had also read Terry's book or he'd come up with the same message on his own, it was still another odd and increasingly irritating coincidence. Either way, it made my synapses misfire, which, in turn, sent my words spluttering off into oblivion. "Um. Ha-ha. That's really very clever," I stammered.

"Who am I? Well, I'm Janice's friend. I'm...I'm more than that, certainly, but in this context that's the important thing."

Idiot, I said to myself.

"What do I want? For you to call me back. That's it, really. That's it for now, I mean. There's a lot more that I want out of *life*, if that's what you're asking, but for right now a quick conversation with you about Janice and her future at XinoniX would make my day. Not that my day is important to you, I understand."

Genius, I said to myself with withering, silent sarcasm. I left my number and signed off.

"I hate voice mail," I said, unrecorded and to no one in particular.

As I left the restaurant, I pulled in a deep draught of the sea air. The Mission Beach area of San Diego is a thin peninsula of land, five or six blocks wide, between the Pacific Ocean and Mission Bay. While the ocean side with its boardwalk and crowds is crazy and chaotic, the bay side is quiet and serene, an ideal place to walk when in a quiet and reflective mood. That's exactly where I found myself, so I crossed Mission Boulevard, cut through the lobby of the Catamaran Hotel, walked out to Mission Bay, and headed south toward my apartment.

Dusk had settled in and sounds of distant laughter and music bounced at me from across the water to remind me that I was spending another Friday evening alone. I think it was Nelson Mandela who said, as he emerged, blinking, into the bright daylight of freedom after spending some ungodly amount of time in solitary confinement, "Loneliness sucks."

In the forty-five minutes it took me to walk home, I managed to spiral myself into a deeply melancholy state of mind. Humming a mournful Hank Williams tune to myself, I unlocked the door and stepped inside. What moved? Was someone in here? "Wishful thinking," I half-joked to myself.

Something brushed against my leg, and I jumped and shouted "HEY!" at a pitch much higher than, in retrospect, I care to admit. In moments like that, the imagination goes into hyperdrive and conjures up all kinds of horrible and grotesque possibilities. The reality, in this case, was just a little brown kitty cat rubbing up against my shin.

Apparently, it had come up the back steps, jumped over the railing, and ventured in through an open window. Now it was meowing at me, as though I owed it a plate of tuna for its re-markable efforts.

"Hey, little kitty," I managed to say in spite of the thunderous pounding in my chest, "you are in a no-animal zone. You trying to get me evicted?" I didn't expect it to answer, and fortunately, it didn't. But when it turned and headed back for the window, I noticed what appeared to be a folded piece of paper taped to its small, brown collar. Instinctively, I bent down for a closer look and there, much to my surprise, written in blue marker was my name. "Fan mail from some flounders?" I said in my best Bullwinkle voice, as I plucked the paper from around her neck.

Relieved of her duty, the little courier jumped up on the win-dow ledge and bolted into the night.

"This is not normal," I muttered to myself as I unfolded the paper. "It's usually a cow that comes through my window to deliver mysterious notes. Or a yak." I sat down at the dining room table, laid the note down, and smoothed out the creases. Two pages.

Dear Steve, the note began in a flowing, pointy script.

> *Please excuse the unorthodox delivery method, but I've never been a subscriber to convention. Earlier this evening you left a message for me; now I have one for you.*

18.

This didn't add up. Forget the apparent fact that Garrison knew who I was, but how the hell did he know where I lived? And what about his seeming preternatural ability with animals, felines, anyway. Was he running some kind of mammalian messenger service?

I ran over to the window where the cat had just perched and peered down into the dark street. Empty. I had hoped, I guess, to see the dark and mysterious silhouette of Teddy Garrison lurking in the shadows of the alley. It wasn't going to be that easy.

I took a deep breath, a decent alternative to letting out an anxious wail, and went back to the table, sat, and read the note at least a dozen times:

> *I know your concern for Janice is heartfelt. I know this because she has told me about you from time to time, and you've always sounded like a good coach and friend, and the two go hand in hand. So I hope you'll understand me when I say that I left XinoniX not for me, but for her.*
>
> *My mentor once said to me that you need to love the people or you'll lose the game. Love, contrary to the popular, romantic notion, is not all hearts and flowers. Love, oftentimes, looks, feels, and hurts like a son of a bitch. Especially in business.*
>
> *I don't only love Janice as she is today; I love what she's capable of becoming. Problem is, she'll never become it as long as I'm around for her to lean on. Janice is the future of the company; she just doesn't*

know it yet. And when I found myself in the position of having more confidence in Janice than she had in herself, I saw my resignation as my ultimate leadership opportunity.

Mostly, leadership requires extreme personal engagement, but sometimes it demands an act of self-removal. This is one of those times. If that makes me look—for the time being, anyway—like a cowardly, selfish schmuck, then so be it.

I know she thinks I've thrown her into the Jeffers den to be eaten alive. Bob has a reputation as a brutal autocrat, and he appears to be the antithesis of the very XinoniX culture that Janice worked so hard to help create. Appearances are misleading.

Jeffers is a brilliant strategist and a superb executive. In other words, he not only plans well, but he also executes the plan, whatever it is, with precision, speed, and focus—all necessary and crucial qualities for the company's next phase. As a leader of people, though, he's awful. That's where Janice comes in.

Janice and Jeffers are perfect for each other and the company. But this is more like an arranged marriage than love at first sight, and I'm the arranger. I would never be able to convince them of their value to each other; they'll have to discover that for themselves. I believe they will. Right now, Janice sees it as a war.

But she doesn't need to conquer Bob, she needs to win him. Help her to see the difference, Steve, and you'll be doing her the favor of a lifetime.

As for me, I hope I've left enough of myself in the

company's DNA, as it were, so that it will continue to evolve in the way I hope and envision.

As for Janice, this is her moment to shine as an Extreme Leader.

As for Jeffers, this is his moment to learn from his weaknesses.

And as for you, Mr. Farber, it's decision time. You need to choose. Are you going to play around or put your skin in the game? That sounds cryptic, I know. Just consider this to be another piece of your own leadership puzzle. You figure out where it fits.

It was signed, simply,

Teddy.

Saturday

19.

That night, I dreamed I was having espresso and maple scones with Teddy Garrison. He was sitting at such an angle that I couldn't clearly see his face, but his profile was familiar, as was the sound of his voice.

"How did you find me?" I was asking the side of his head.

"That's the wrong question," he mumbled through a mouthful of pastry, spraying a few crumbs for emphasis.

"What's the right question?" I asked.

"That is," said Ted the dream.

I awoke on Saturday morning to the sound of thunder. As it turned out, it wasn't thunder, exactly, but someone pounding on my door. I did my best to ignore the intruder, who was doing his best to make sure that he couldn't be ignored. I shook the cobwebs from my dream-filled brain and fumbled for my jean shorts, which were positioned strategically in a pile on the floor next to my bed.

I stumbled through the apartment and past the table where the note still lay, rippling slightly in a breeze wafting in through the open window. As I yanked the door open, I expected to see Bruce, the landlord, who lived upstairs, or maybe a cat with a telegram. It was neither.

"Morning, Sunshine," said Edg.

"You're not a cat," I said.

"Nowadays we say dude," he said, without missing a beat.

"Don't take this the wrong way," I said, "but what the hell are you doing here?"

He held up a white bag in his left hand. "Sustenance," he said as he pushed past me. I followed him into my own apartment.

He put the bag on the table next to Garrison's note and started poking around the kitchen. "Where do you keep the morning elixir?"

I ground some mocha java beans, and Edg filled the coffee-pot with purified water from the jug on the counter. The apartment filled with a beautiful, caffeinated aroma, and my head, finally, began to clear itself of the murky effects of dream, sleep, and rude awakening.

We sat facing each other across the table. "Here's the question of the day, Edg."

"Fire away."

"I've never told you where I live, so how did you find me?"

"Why is that the question of the day?"

"Long story. Answer, please."

He opened the little white bag and pulled out a chocolate croissant. "I'm going to let you in on a little secret." He tore the pastry into two and handed me the bigger piece. I took the offering and leaned forward in my chair.

He paused, as if contemplating whether or not to let me in on his special technique. "It's like this," he said, locking his eyes on mine. "*You're in the phone book, dude!*"

He let out a loud guffaw, obviously in response to the disappointed look on my face. The mystery had evaporated in a puff.

He opened the bag again and placed a fresh scone on the table. Given the dream I'd just had, this was a Rod Serling moment.

"That's not maple, is it?"

"Blueberry. Here, take half."

"No thanks. I'm not in a scone mood."

"C'mon, take it. I never scone alone." I obliged.

A gust blew through the window, and Garrison's note fluttered off the table and landed near my feet. I picked it up, folded it, and slid it under my coffee cup. I was trying to be inconspicuous, but I let my gaze linger just a little too long.

"Writing love notes?" Edg grinned. "Or getting them?"

"Neither," I said curtly, hoping he'd drop the inquisition. I didn't want to explain this odd note and the odd circumstances around it. I couldn't. It made very little sense, at least in the normal, rational sort of way that things are supposed to. But then neither did Edg nor the circumstances around him, me, Pops, and, most recently, Smitty. *So, what the hell*, I figured.

I told Edg the whole story starting with Janice's phone call. I talked about my visit to her office, her challenge with Jeffers, and her subsequent epiphany about the purpose of her work. I told how she'd asked me to find this Garrison guy, and how he'd found me instead. I told about the cat, the note—I waved the evidence in the air for emphasis—and even the dream. He stopped chewing and looked down at his half-eaten scone.

"Hmm," he offered. He tapped his fingers on the table. "Should we play twenty questions, or are you gonna let me read the note?"

I handed it to him, and he took his time soaking it in. He read it silently two or three times, stopped, gazed up at the ceiling, looked at me, and read it again.

"Well?" I prompted.

Edg folded the note, handed it back to me, and shoved the last piece of scone into his mouth. "Awesome," he said with a mouthful. "Let's go."

He jumped up and headed for the door. I, of course, followed.

20.

This field trip brought us into the Point Loma neighborhood of San Diego: old money residents, brick-and-mortar houses, and tree-lined streets. Following Edg's directions, I curbed the Mustang in front of an impressive Tudor-style home. Deep green vines of ivy formed an archway over its stained-glass door.

"Guess where we are," said Edg.

"No clue."

"I'll give you one: 'Go to the source and ask the horse, he'll give you the answer that you endorse,'" he sang. "'That is, of course, unless the horse is the famous...'" He left the melody hanging and waited for me to finish it.

"Mister Ed?" I said. "Mister Ed the talking horse lives here?"

"Close. How about Mr. Ted?"

"Come again?"

"This, my good man," he said, slipping into a mock British accent, "is the illustrious domicile of one Theodore 'Teddy' Garrison, man of mystery."

"Teddy Garrison? You know Teddy Garrison?"

"He and my Pops are very close."

"The mentor that Garrison referred to in his note?"

"That'd be Pops."

I sat slack jawed with my hands still on the wheel. "Wait a minute," I said, feeling a sudden gurgle of irritation. "Why didn't you tell me that earlier?"

Edg vaulted over the convertible door. "You want to talk to him or not?"

"Yeah, I want to talk to him. But you..."

"Move it or lose it, now or never, you snooze you lose," he called back over his shoulder as he strode up the cobblestone walk.

"Wait!" I called after him. "Shouldn't we call first?"

Edg stopped at the porch and turned back to me. "Oh, well, by all means," he said with a withering British snarl. "That approach has worked famously thus far."

I couldn't argue with that, so I joined him at the front door.

I rang the bell. A dog barked. I knocked. Another bark. We waited. I shuffled my feet. I rang again. The dog obliged again. "Not home," I said, trying to conceal my relief.

"Or not answering," said Edg as he squinted through the near opaque stained glass. "Let's go around back."

To my dismay, he took off across the yard and disappeared around the side of the house. I looked around for the cops.

"Hey!" I stage-whispered after him. "What are you doing?"

I took a quick inventory of my choices: I could stand there and shuffle my feet like an idiot, I could jump back in the car and get the hell out of there, or I could swallow my paranoia and pursue Edg in his trespass.

"Oh, shit," I hissed, as I dashed across the yard and felt the little hairs on the back of my neck prickling in angst. I pushed through a thick hedge of fragrant jasmine and emerged into a lush, perfectly manicured landscape. A black wrought iron fence trimmed the perimeter of a perfect kelly green lawn. In the center of the yard stood a hardwood gazebo, and in the center of the gazebo stood Edg. He waved me over, so I walked up the steps and joined him on the platform. He looked over at the house with a slight, almost wistful, smile.

"Nice place, huh?" he said. "Yeah. Striking. Now let's go."

"Nah. Chill out. It's okay for us to hang here a while. Nobody will mind." He leaned against the railing. "Now let's talk about that note."

By this time, I wasn't sure I believed in coincidences, but, for lack of an alternative explanation, I had slipped the note into my back pocket as we left my apartment. Registering no hint of surprise, Edg took the note from me and scanned it again like he had at my kitchen table.

"What do you make of this?" he asked.

"Well, he seems to be explaining, or justifying, his decision to leave XinoniX." I thought for a moment. "And that's really interesting, considering he didn't have to explain *anything* to me. He doesn't even know me."

"You spent a little time with my friend, Smitty, yesterday."

"Yeah…what's that got to do with it?"

"Learn anything?"

"Uh…read the signs?"

"Read the signs." He held up the note. "What does this sign say to you?"

"What do you mean?"

"I mean, what if this had nothing, ultimately, to do with Janice, Jeffers, XinoniX, or Garrison? What if it were written entirely for your benefit?"

"For my benefit? That's nuts. It makes no sense."

"Oh, well, sure. There's nothing nuts about this at all. Other than the fact that it was delivered by a cat," he sneered. "When did making sense become an important criterion in this bizarre little scenario of yours?"

"Touché," I said.

"Now," he said, "read the sign."

I read the note again, the romantic in me half-expecting to see it radiate with a mysterious, unearthly, sign-worthy glow. But I saw the same words, the same paper, and the same tight, normal human script.

"I'm not getting anything," I said, rubbing my thumb between my eyes. "The psychic hotline must be down again."

"Uh-huh," he said, clearly unamused. "Let's try another approach. Put it down."

I folded the note and slipped it back into my pocket.

"Garrison wrote this to you because you contacted him, right?"

I nodded.

"And you contacted Garrison because Janice asked you to find him?"

I nodded again.

"And why did she come to you in the first place?"

"Because she values me as a counselor, I guess."

"More than you do," said Edg.

"Beg your pardon?"

"It seems to me that she has a greater belief in your abilities than you do."

"That sounds familiar," I said, as I fished around for the note.

"Leave it," he said. "It's not going anywhere." I complied. "Think about what happened in her office the other day. What was going on with her?"

"Well," I recalled, "she was dispirited, disheartened, and ready to quit her job."

"And you helped rekindle her fire, didn't you?"

"I can't take credit for that."

"What can you take credit for?"

"I guess I just asked the right question?" He looked at me. "I asked the right question," I said, turning it into a statement.

"Which was?"

"Which was, 'Why do you love your job?'"

"Now, how about asking the right question for you?"

"How about you giving me a clue." I was getting impatient. I felt myself chafe, as if I were developing an emotional rash.

"Okay. Here's one. Do you know what the word *audacious* means?"

"You mean audacious as in LEAP?"

"That's the one. Audacity is a bold and blatant disregard for normal constraints. But if you look it up in *Webster's Thesaurus*, you'll see that it has a couple of connotations. One is audacity as it relates to courage, and the other is the audacity synonymous with impudence, temerity, or brazenness."

"I bet you were a lit major."

He chuckled at himself, "I try to do my homework. But the difference between the two meanings," he went on, "comes down to love versus ego. Love-inspired audacity is courageous and bold and filled with valor. It's the kind of audacity that's required to change the world for the better. Ego-inspired audacity is just a pain in the ass. In other words, some people are audacious just for the purpose of drawing attention to themselves; they're not concerned about anything other than their image."

"Is that my clue? Are you calling me a pain in the ass?" I was kidding, I hoped.

"That depends."

"On what?"

"Did you go to Janice's office out of love and compassion for her and her predicament or because it would look good on your résumé as an executive coach?"

"I didn't even think about my résumé," I said, sounding, I'm sure, as defensive as I felt. "And I'm not even getting paid for this."

"Hey," Edg laughed, "I believe you. So if love is your motivation for helping her, what are you trying to accomplish?"

"I'd like her to be happier in her job and be a better leader for her company."

Edg stepped back from the gazebo's railing, closed his eyes, stretched his arms way above his head, and let out a thunderous yawn. The dog barked inside Garrison's house. I gaped at Edg.

"I'm sorry," I scowled. "Am I keeping you from your nappy time?"

"Sorry, dude. No offense, but that's just so…normal," said Edg as he boosted himself up and sat on the gazebo's railing. He let his legs swing under him. He reminded me of a little kid sitting on a swing at the playground. "This time," he said, "I want to hear some audacity, dude! *What are you trying to accomplish*?"

"I want to help Janice reenergize her company?"

"Are you asking me or telling me? C'mon, quit screwing around."

"Okay," I gave in. "Let me give it an earnest try. What I want to accomplish, audaciously speaking, is —" I waited for the appropriate inspiring words to spring forth from my lips. Waiting for inspiring words, I've noticed, all but guarantees they won't show up.

"What?"

"I want to help Janice save the human race." I felt my cheeks flush, and I immediately started searching for a different, less embarrassing answer. It sounded too cliché, too Hallmark Card, too Successories. The problem was I meant it. Janice's mission, I realized, had struck a chord with me. I wanted a piece of her legacy. I wanted to be able to say that I played a significant role in changing the world, and not because it would look good on my résumé. Even though it would.

Edg grinned. "There you go. You want to change the world by helping to save the human race. Now, if you take that intent seriously and give it the thought it deserves, you'll think of thousands of ways you can use your talent to do it. But for now, helping Janice is a damned good place to start, it seems to me."

I noticed myself nodding in agreement, even though hesitation and doubt still showed on my face. "It still seems a little abstract to me. I don't want it to, Edg, but it does. Maybe it comes from years of conditioning in the business world. Words like *trust* and *love*, and phrases like *change the world*, even though I know they're important, are usually scoffed at and dismissed as soft."

"Who dismisses them?"

"Well, the hard-core, no-nonsense business types, mostly."

"Those days are over." Edg took off his shades and wiped them between the folds of his Tommy Bahama shirt. "The sun is setting on those so-called hard-core types. All you have to do is look at the stock market in the wake of Enron, Andersen, WorldCom, ImClone, and Tyco—remember them?—followed by the Madoff debacle, the subprime blowup, the bank bailouts, and the Wall Street meltdown. All you have to do is watch your 401(k) evaporate with your retirement dreams, and you'll see that trust and love and values are anything but touchy-feely. Now, even the average guy on the street knows that integrity and his bank account are intimately connected. Trust and love and humanity are hard-core business principles. The posers have been exposed; the Extreme Leaders are going to emerge.

"This will be the age of love-inspired audacity," he continued, picking up a full head of steam. "Now is the time for all of us to take our power back and become, each of us, Extreme Leaders in our own right. We have to set a new example of what's right in business and everywhere else. We have to be audacious enough to follow the examples we respect and challenge the ones we don't.

"An underling who shreds suspect documents because the boss told her to do it is choosing to be just that, an underling. That person is making a conscious choice to perpetuate rotten leadership and is, therefore, a party to it. "But if that underling looks into her own heart, finds the values that reside there and summons the audacity to do what's right and honorable, she chooses to reject the boss's order and take the consequences, she has then stepped into the role of Extreme Leader, and by her stance contributes to the creation of a better world. I wonder what would have happened at Andersen if more of their consultants had made that choice."

"Wait a minute," I said. "Andersen had great people; I know a lot of them personally. They lost their jobs because of a few idiots at the top. It's not fair to put the blame on the accountants and office workers."

"Okay. Maybe the outcome for Andersen wouldn't have

changed. We'll never know. But I do know this: It's very easy to sit back and point the accusing finger at a few number perverse thugs at the top. Very easy. We're all doing a lot of finger-pointing these days, and even though a few bad guys are going to the slammer, that doesn't solve much in our own lives."

"All right, Edg," I said, "I hear you. But let's say you're talking to your average, everyday corporate employee or supervisor. Or manager. What will you say to them?"

"Average is a pejorative."

"You know what I mean."

"I'd tell them the same thing I'm telling you, make a commitment, right now, that no matter where you sit on the org chart, no matter what it says in your job description, stand up for what's right and normal constraints be damned.

"The world needs you right now. The world needs your influence and your audacious action. Your actions will require you to find strength in your heart. Never let anyone tell you that your heart's not big enough, and don't believe the hype that the world is controlled by a select few. Nobody controls your world unless you choose to let them.

"Take a stand; put your skin in the game; advocate for integrity. This is the time to shift the image, behavior, and, ultimately, the legacy of business, and you do that through your own behavior and example.

"You may not think you can change the Whole World that we live in—and you may be wrong—but you can certainly change the world—small *w*—that you and yours live in: the world of your company, the world of your employees, the world of your industry, or the world of your family. To deny that is to deny your capability as a human being.

"But, hey...it's your choice."

Just then I heard a phone ring inside the house. The answering machine clicked on, and a familiar message drifted through an open window on the second floor and, it seemed, spoke to me through the breeze: "*Who are you and what do you want?*" A bead of sweat rolled down my back. The caller hung up.

Edg was grinning; I wasn't.

21.

Bob Jeffers was in the hospital. He had collapsed at the office on Saturday at the same time, it turns out, that Edg was grilling me at Garrison's gazebo. At first they thought it was a heart attack, but it proved to be some kind of stress-related panic attack. Janice had ridden with him to the hospital, which was only fair because she was the one who had flattened him.

Saturday at XinoniX is a peaceful time. A few people with pressing deadlines will show up in their shorts and flip-flops to work without the distractions of a typical weekday. This Saturday, however, the office was empty. At least Janice thought it was. Bob Jeffers thought so too. They worked in their own self-contained offices, absorbed in their tasks, each blissfully unaware of the other, when Mama Nature, in her infinite humor, set off their biological pagers at precisely the same moment.

Janice put down her pen. Jeffers pushed away from his computer. Janice stepped into her hallway. Jeffers pulled his door shut and locked it. Janice turned right, Jeffers, left. They sprinted toward the bathroom, rounded the blind corner from opposite directions, and smacked right into each other.

The shock was too much for Bob: he clutched his chest and fell over backwards, cracking his head on the wall on the way down. A less honorable person in Janice's shoes might have seen the situation as an opportunity to let her corporate adversary expire before her eyes, strains of "Ding-Dong! The Witch is Dead" chiming cheerily in her head. But Janice lunged for the nearest phone and called 911. Then she rode in the ambulance and, I've been told, held The 51% Guy's hand all the way to the hospital.

Adversity, someone once said, doesn't build character; it reveals it.

We had been camped in Garrison's backyard for so long that I was beginning to feel at home on that gazebo. That was odd, considering I hadn't met our host.

As usual, Edg had given me a lot to think about, and I was feeling emotionally provoked, intellectually stimulated, and physically exhausted. My cell phone chirped and I apologized to Edg as I answered. Janice filled me in on the scene at the hospital and on the events that had brought her there. Edg listened in on my end of the conversation.

"You're where? What happened? Really? You're kidding. Is he all right? Why do you want me there? Well, sure, I suppose I could come if that's what you really want. I'll be there as soon as I can." I rang off and looked at Edg.

"Garrison and I will have to meet some other day," I said. "Duty calls. I have to go to the hospital."

"Everything okay?" he asked.

"Seems so. That was Janice, she's in the hospital with Bob Jeffers." I gave him the quick sketch. "She says she wants to have a heart-to-heart with him right now."

"Sounds like your opportunity," he said, pushing his small, dark shades up the bridge of his nose.

"For what?"

"That's for you to know and you to find out."

I didn't have the time, energy, or patience to pursue that one.

Edg told me that he was going to hang around for a while, and, over my protests, he convinced me to go directly to the hospital.

"Don't worry about me," he said. "I'll find my way home."

As I cut back through the hedge and around the side of the house, the dog barked again, and, to my surprise, I heard the back door open and shut.

I turned around and sprinted back to the yard. Edg was gone.

"Sonofabitch," I said to myself. "Garrison was in there the whole time."

As I opened the door to the Mustang, I happened to glance back at the house, and for a moment it seemed that the house was looking back at me. But it wasn't the house; it was two pairs of eyes in the upstairs window, one belonging to a little brown kitty cat, and the other to a dog. A retriever. And it sure as hell looked a lot like Sadie.

22.

I was anxious. It was visiting hours at Sharp Hospital, so getting into Jeffers's room wouldn't be a problem. I had no idea what to expect once I did, though. Janice was counting on me for something. To facilitate, she'd said. That's one of those loaded words that means different things to different people. I knew some facilitators who would be showing up right now with a box of mango-scented markers and a pad of flipchart paper. I didn't think that's what Janice had in mind.

I had no pens or paper, but I had other advantages: (1) I had worked with Jeffers before, and, as far as I could tell, he liked me well enough. (2) I had, it goes without saying, a great relationship with Janice, and, for some reason, she trusted me. And (3)—this was the big one—I wanted to help Jeffers, Janice, and XinoniX save the world.

I don't know if I was romanticizing or blowing this way out of proportion, but it suddenly occurred to me that the stakes were enormous. And right then, with my hand resting on the door handle as I hesitated in the hallway outside of Jeffers's room, I felt as though some significant piece of the future would be determined in the next few minutes. The livelihood, and perhaps lives, of a lot of people were unknowingly dependent on the outcome of the imminent conversation. XinoniX's future would depend on both Janice and Jeffers staying there, and staying there to work together. And their staying there would somehow depend on me.

And right then, in that moment, two words came to mind.

Janice was sitting in a chair in a corner of the otherwise vacant room. The bed was empty, and there was no sign of Jeffers as she stood up to greet me. She was wearing shorts and a tank top, Saturday work clothes, and her red eyes were a sharp contrast to the pallor of her face. Janice looked whipped.

"Is he dead?" I asked, trying in my own perverted way to lighten the mood with a bit of gallows humor.

"That's not funny," said Janice with a scowl. "For a minute I thought I'd killed him, and believe me, there wasn't an ounce of humor in the situation. Turns out it was just some kind of panic attack, that and a pretty good bump on the head, but it scared the living hell out of me."

"Sorry," I said. "I'm a little uneasy myself, I guess. So where is he?"

"Bathroom."

"Think he made it this time?"

Janice laughed in spite of herself. Gallows humor sometimes misses the mark, but relentless gallows humor will eventually nail the bull's-eye.

"So, what's the plan?" I asked.

"Basically, I just wanted you here for moral support, to hold my hand, emotionally speaking, while I do what I have to do."

"Which is what?"

"Resign."

"Oh shit," I started to say, but I didn't get the chance, because just then the door swung open and an orderly wheeled Bob Jeffers into the room.

Janice may have looked bad, but next to Jeffers she was fresh as a springtime daisy. His skin was gray, and his thick salt-and-pepper hair was sticking up from behind a gauze bandage. Stocky white legs jutted out from under the hospital-issue gown, and his feet were tucked into black calf-length GoldToe socks. His legendary fifty-one-percent blowhard bravado had run up against his own mortality and nearly been overruled. When he saw me, his eyes sparked with quizzical recognition.

"Steve Farber, right? It's been a long time."

"Hi Bob," I said, extending my hand into empty space. "How are you feeling?"

He glanced at Janice, then back at me, and took my floating hand in his surprisingly strong grasp.

"Lucky. I'm feeling lucky. New lease on life and all that," he sighed. "But, and I don't mean to be impolite, what are you doing here?"

"I asked him to come," said Janice before I could reply. "If you're feeling up to it, I thought the three of us could talk."

The orderly helped Jeffers back onto the bed, said "Fifteen minutes left of visiting hours," and slipped out of the room. We looked at each other in uncomfortable silence. Janice and I sat, and Jeffers picked up a paper cup and munched thoughtfully on a mouthful of shaved ice.

"We know you need to rest," I said to Jeffers. "So if you'd rather do this later, I'd certainly understand." I was hoping, frankly, for a response that would liberate me from this place. I never liked hospitals. Or conflict. Conflict in a hospital was a double whammy that I was sure I could live without.

He swallowed and said, "I don't know what you want to talk about, but I suppose I can take anything for fourteen minutes."

But who's counting?

Janice cleared her throat conspicuously, and we both looked over to her. *Here we go*, I thought.

"Bob," she began. "I think it's time for me to—"

"Put things on the table," I butted in. "That's why she asked me here. To see if I could help you guys sort things out." I knew it wasn't polite to talk over another person, at least that's what they taught in facilitator school, but sometimes the end did justify the means. I barged ahead before Janice could recover from the shock of my intrusion. Only thirteen minutes left. No time for subtlety. I took a deep breath.

"Bob," I said, "do you know that everyone at your company thinks you're a jerk?" I heard Janice gasp. "Your employees and executives, including Janice, think you're an autocratic, uncaring, out of touch bureaucrat who doesn't give a rat's ass about the future of XinoniX."

He stopped chomping on his ice. No turning back now, I thought.

"But," I said, before he could get a word in, "I have it on good authority—Garrison, as a matter of fact—that it's not true." I shot a looked at an addled Janice. "It's an unfortunate misperception of who you really are and what you really want."

Now both of their mouths were hanging open. Mine kept moving.

I turned to Janice. "Let me tell you what Garrison says. He says that Bob is a brilliant strategist. He says that Bob's abilities to analyze and execute are second to none and that XinoniX would have no future without him."

"When did you find Teddy?" gasped Janice.

I ignored the question. "But you already know that, don't you, Bob?"

He looked at the floor, hesitated, and said, "Yes."

Janice trembled with anger. But before she could call him an arrogant prick or something less flowery, I forged on. "But you also know something else, right?"

"Yes," he said. "Yes, I do."

"What?" shouted Janice.

He turned his head and, for the first time that I'd noticed, looked her in the eye. He said, "I suck at the people thing. But you're a superstar in that department. I can't do this without you, without your influence."

Her jaw dropped again, and I saw in her eyes that she was frantically trying to process this new information.

"Listen," he said. "I know that what Steve says is true. I've tried hard to deny it, I admit, but this experience," he waved his hand around to indicate his hospital room, "has been a wake-up call, to borrow a phrase."

"How so?" I asked.

"I'm stressed out. I'm not sure that I can live up to everyone's expectations of me. When I took over for Garrison I knew I was stepping into a business that he built, in large part, with his personality and charisma." He paused, sighed again. "Not my strong suits. Don't get me wrong, I'm a good businessman. I've got a successful track record. I'm proud of what I've done in my life, but Teddy's a tough act to follow. People not only respect him, they love him. From what you've told me, and, like I said, I already know it, I'm not scoring very high on either of those measures."

"Do you regret taking the job?" I asked, surprised by his candor.

He looked around the room. "Remains to be seen. I regret that something about it made me end up here, that's for sure."

"Why'd you take the job in the first place?"

"The rumor is that the board hired me and forced Teddy out, but that's not true. He recruited me. He told me the XinoniX story, laid out the vision and the challenges, and appealed to what he called my unequaled business acumen. That was a nice compliment, but that's not why I signed up."

Janice was mute. I asked, "Why did you?"

"I saw it as my opportunity to do something significant for the world."

I felt my skin tingle. "Do what for the world?"

He hesitated, looked down at his hands. "Save it," he whispered.

"Meaning?"

Another hesitation. "Well...this may sound strange coming from me, but I've come to appreciate that there's more to business than numbers. Yes, numbers are important, to say the least, and I'm a master when it comes to that. And there's no doubt that when the numbers are good we get paid accordingly. I've hit my share of numbers in my life, and I've been rewarded well for doing it. But I've had this growing, persistent feeling that something vital's been missing."

"Like what?" asked Janice.

"I've had a hard time putting it into words. Soul? Meaning? Impact? Don't know, exactly." He looked my way. "I once heard your pal, Tom Peters, say that his nightmare is to have his tombstone read, 'He made budget.' I can relate to that. I want my legacy to mean something. So I joined XinoniX to do something important, and I figured that if I could do that, the numbers would follow."

"So, what do you want on your tombstone, Bob?" I asked with a wry allusion to the pizza commercial.

"He *helped.*"

Janice looked stunned. "Why didn't you ever say this to me, Bob?"

"Never said it to anybody."

"Why not?"

Bob shrugged.

"Bob?" said Janice.

"Yeah?"

"You suck at the people thing."

Bob's shoulders shook, and I heard a sound that I'd never heard from him before. He was laughing.

"That's what I need you for, Janice. Would you help me with that?"

She looked up at the ceiling and drew in a deep breath. "Sign me up," she said.

"Okay," I said, getting up out of my chair. "Seems like the two of you have a common agenda after all. Aren't you glad we had this little chat?" It was a question that required no answer.

"Now there's something else you guys gotta do."

"What?" they asked in unison.

"Prove you mean it."

Sunday

23.

Janice was on her way to my apartment. I had promised her an explanation about Garrison as we'd stood in the hospital parking lot after yesterday's encounter. I'd put her off, invoking fatigue and near brain death.

I had stopped at the supermarket on the way home and bought myself a Saturday night recuperation kit: a liter of Diet Coke, a frozen pizza—guess which kind—a container of Ben and Jerry's Cherry Garcia, and a tub of Cool Whip. One of the cable stations was running a *Twilight Zone* marathon, which, for some reason, seemed appropriate.

So now, on this bright Sunday morning, I drank my coffee and nursed an all-out sugar and fat hangover, while I tried to collect my thoughts and achieve enough brainwave coherence to explain to Janice my sort of encounter with Garrison. I wasn't having much success.

I read the Sunday comics and found myself pining for a new *Far Side* cartoon. Gary Larson's cows always had a way of putting things in perspective. I thought of the one where a man-cow was sitting in his easy chair reading the paper.

His wife-cow wore a designer dress and dangly earrings and

held a glass of wine in her hoof. She gazed wistfully out the window of their beautiful, palatial home and said, "Wendell, I'm not content."

I often think of that cartoon. Must be a sign.

I stepped out on the balcony and looked down on the street just as Janice pulled into a parking space across the way. As she stepped out of her Pathfinder, I happened to glance up the street to my left and saw Edg coming toward her on his skateboard. He saw Janice and screeched to a halt, flipping his board up and grabbing it in his hand. He didn't seem to panic, exactly, but he looked around as if trying to calculate an escape route. He jumped back on his board and took off to his right down the alley behind the neighboring apartment building. Gone. Edg didn't strike me as the type to engage in wimpy avoidance behavior, but it sure looked like that's what he'd just done.

Janice, oblivious to the scene, slipped her keys into her purse and crossed the street toward me. "Hey!" she called up to me. "Can I come up?"

We sat on a couple of tall stools that I had strategically positioned on the balcony to afford a view of the sparkling bay. A soft breeze rustled the fronds of my old friend, Mr. Palm. Another perfect San Diego Sunday, that is, except for my dull sugar headache.

"Okay," she said, "dish."

I produced the note and handed it to her, figuring that that would communicate the essence of the situation. I had neither the desire nor the energy to spell out the whole scenario in detail.

"A note straight from the horse's mouth," I said, mixing a metaphor like others would a martini.

She scrunched up her eyebrows as her gaze zigzagged

through the script. "I don't understand that man. Why wouldn't he just call and talk to me about this?"

"Seemed pretty clear to me," I said. "He wants you to grow without his help. Consider yourself weaned from the leadership teat of Teddy Garrison." God, I love metaphors.

"Okay, but he…"

"Forget about him for the time being, Janice. Garrison helped to get you this far but you're the one who has to make the leap, you know?"

"What if I can't?"

"Well, here's what my friend, Edg, would tell you."

"Who?"

"That's a whole other story for another time. Anyway, he'd say that your love for XinoniX, its products, and its people will give you the energy to be audacious, bold, and courageous. If you keep reminding yourself and others about the importance of your work, about the great future you're striving to create, you'll generate the energy you need to work through any obstacle and challenge. Your energy will be contagious to others, including Jeffers, just as Garrison's was to you.

"I saw your lights go on, Janice. I saw it the other morning in your office, I saw it yesterday at the hospital, and I see it now. Love generates energy. That's the simple truth. You already know it, consciously or not. You may think you're still vacillating on your leadership role, but your heart has already committed to the cause."

"You sound pretty sure about that."

"I am."

"How can you be more convinced about me than I am?"

"Doesn't have to be that way. You're just missing one last step."

"Which is?"

"Love requires proof. You have to prove it to yourself and you have to prove it to everyone around you."

"How?"

"Let's start with *when*."

"Okay, then, when?"

I had already given this a lot of thought. "Is Jeffers going to work tomorrow?"

"So he told me."

"Are you? Because that would be a requirement in this whole leadership thing."

"Ha-ha. Yes, I'm going to work. You heard me promise Bob that I'd stay."

"Okay. Tomorrow, then. Let's give XinoniX a reason to celebrate the coming of Monday."

"That'd be a switch," she said.

"Well...you need a switch to turn on the lights." Now that was a good metaphor, straight from the horse's teat.

We spent the next couple of hours putting our plan together, and by the time we'd finished, both Janice and I felt that Monday had the potential to be the start of not only a new week, but also of a new, re-energized XinoniX. As afternoon tilted toward evening, Janice headed off to brief Jeffers on his role in Monday's events and to make sure he was on board. I pulled on a sweatshirt and headed out for a stroll; it was all up to them now.

I paused at the end of the walkway and looked up at my old friend, Mr. Palm. For the first time in a long while, I didn't feel the need for a smack on the head to get me to think clearly. I was feeling pretty good about my new perspective on my life and my work.

I had always liked it when people asked me what I did for work, and I answered proudly with labels like *leadership coach, consultant, seminar leader,* or *speaker*. It was different, even glamorous, and always made for interesting and lively conversation. But what had dawned on me with increasing brilliance over the past few days was the disturbing realization that the roles I played were fundamentally empty and nearly devoid of meaning. It all sounded great, but I hadn't really strived to do anything of lasting significance. I had been working with leaders, but I hadn't been leading. I had spoken with conviction, but I hadn't been convinced. I had inspired a few people to action, but I hadn't, when I looked at my work with cold, objective scrutiny, done diddly do.

It was different now. Fundamentally altered. I was falling in love with my job or, more accurately, I was quitting my job and taking up a calling. Not that I was anything special, not by any measure, but I was, at last, crystal-clear about what I wanted to accomplish in my time on this planet. And when I thought about this newfound mission to change whatever part of the world I touched, I felt a real, authentic, warmth stirring in my heart. Love, to put it simply.

As I allowed myself the indulgence of this wonderful feeling, I noticed that I really didn't care if my thoughts sounded like the text of a Hallmark card. From this day forward, I vowed to myself as I stood there under the tree, with every bit of energy and audacity I could muster I would approach my life and every client engagement with the expressed intent of transforming the world. And if I fell short of the mark or even failed completely, I wouldn't have the slightest residue of regret because my intent would always be noble. I was leaping, damn it. And it was exhilarating.

Even though I had been working a long time in the leadership arena, my encounter with Janice, Jeffers, and XinoniX felt like a beginning. Would they turn things around over there? I didn't know. Would Janice be a considerably better leader as a result of the effort? Most assuredly so. I had no doubt that she would go on to do astoundingly great things, regardless of what would, or wouldn't, happen tomorrow. And that felt…well, totally awesome, dude.

As I got ready for bed that evening, it occurred to me that aside from the odd, distant glimpse from my balcony, I hadn't seen Edg since I'd left him Saturday afternoon on Garrison's gazebo. I really liked the guy, so I'm not embarrassed to admit that I kind of missed him. Our conversations had had a remarkable effect on the way I was thinking about the world and my place in it. And in our very brief time together, I had fallen into a deep well of gratitude for him and his insights. He'd asked for nothing in return yet, for some reason, I'd never questioned his motives. At our second meeting, he had said that I'd be doing him a great favor, but I'd seen no evidence of that. Maybe he'd just wanted someone to pick on.

I flicked on the TV and tuned in to the local evening news in time to see the weather forecast. In San Diego, there's not much drama in the climate story. The coastal temperature highs and lows average seventy or so; tack on another ten to twenty degrees, and there's your inland temperature. That's the whole story.

In other words, the weather report didn't demand a lot of focus, so I almost missed the story that came next. The name, William Maritime, snapped my attention back to the TV like a bungee cord on a bridge jumper.

The anchor was saying, "The reclusive multimillionaire and philanthropist died late this afternoon at San Diego Memorial Hospital. The cause of death has not been confirmed, but sources close to the late Mr. Maritime tell us that he had been battling cancer for some time. He had spent his final days quietly in a mobile home in North County, San Diego. Here's Jennifer Lee with a retrospective on the widely loved, deeply respected, and some would say, mysterious businessman."

I sat on the edge of my bed, as my heart fell to my stomach and flopped around as though it were drowning in there. No wonder I hadn't seen Edg today.

"Oh man," I said out loud. "Oh man, oh man, oh man."

I had no way to reach Edg. I had no idea where he lived; and I had a crushing fear that I wouldn't see him again for a long time.

I fished around in my pocket for the note that Pops had given me just a couple of days, it seemed like eons, earlier. I held in my hands the only tangible evidence that I had, in fact, spent a few miraculous hours with the great man and that he, justified or not, had decided to believe in me. Now he was gone. The written word always outlasts the man.

This note, I knew, would be the fuel I would run on for the rest of my life. It had taken Pops a few minutes to write it; it would power me forever. I read it over and over until the words were etched in my brain and, certainly, on my heart. I closed my eyes and watched the words fall and float in the darkness behind my eyelids. My heart stopped.

Frantic, I pulled Garrison's note from the other pocket of my jean shorts and held the two scripts side by side. And then everything fell into place with a resounding click.

Monday

24.

Monday morning at XinoniX started earlier than usual for Janice and Jeffers. They had met in the office at six thirty and polished the agenda for the companywide meeting, which had been called for 10 a.m. I arrived at nine, got my visitor's pass, and waited for the two of them in the executive conference room.

I hadn't heard from Edg, and I found it hard to think of anything else, so I did what I normally do when I'm feeling agitated and distracted: I paced. My eyes wandered along the conference room walls. They provided a kind of visual history of the company. On one wall was a gallery of framed XinoniX marketing brochures and articles from the *Wall Street Journal*, *Barron's*, *Fortune*, *Forbes*, and several other business publications. On the other was picture after picture of the XinoniX gang from various parties and company events. The biggest and most conspicuous picture was a group shot with a caption that read, *All of Us*. Because I'd never seen a picture of Garrison, I wanted to try and pick him out in the crowd. But before I could get close enough to see the photo clearly, Janice and Bob came through the door.

They looked good, and I heard something approaching nervous cheer in their voices as they bid me good morning. Bob was wearing khaki pants and a soft, black sport coat over a white silk T-shirt, his head bandage replaced by an oversized Band-Aid. Janice wore a XinoniX logo polo shirt tucked into her usual crisp-pressed designer jeans. I was glad I had opted for the casual look myself, mainly because I had woken up too late and been far too tired to wrestle with a necktie.

"Showtime," said Janice as she beckoned me to the door. The XinoniX crowd was already gathering in the cafeteria when we made our entrance. I helped myself to a cup of coffee and a bagel as Bob and Janice circulated through the room, shaking hands and making small talk.

As I stood at the table and dumped creamer and Equal in my cup, I overheard a couple of people (I always learn a lot when I'm anonymous) offering each other their take on the upcoming proceedings.

"This should be interesting," said the guy with the cranberry muffin. "I don't think I've heard Jeffers say a single word since he's been here."

"Yeah, *interesting*," said the woman with the fruit plate. "I've seen this kind of crap a hundred times. The last thing I need is a bunch of rah rah crap. At my last company, we had a town hall meeting every week. It was always empty condescending crap. I have too much crap to do to spend my time listening to a bunch of crap from people who don't really give a crap about me."

"Yeah," said Muffin Man. "I hear ya."

I took a sip of my coffee, and for some reason it tasted like crap.

I sat at the back of the room so I could get the widest possible perspective of the group. I sipped and munched while the cafeteria filled up. Janice stepped to the front and thumped the microphone.

"Can you hear me okay?"

I nodded my head vigorously, put down my cup, and gave her an enthusiastic thumbs-up.

"Please have a seat and we'll get started in a few minutes."

"Oh, hooray," someone muttered.

I looked to my left. It was Crap Lady, sitting right next to me. What a great opportunity for an attitudinal experiment.

"Excuse me," I said. "I was thinking about getting some fruit. How is it?"

"Not too bad," she said through a mouthful. "But this is California; kinda hard to screw up fruit in California."

I had a feeling that was high praise, coming from her. "This coffee tastes like crap," I offered.

"Always does," she said.

Surprise, surprise, I thought.

The murmuring in the cafeteria subsided as Jeffers took a seat facing the crowd and Janice returned to the mic.

"Good morning!" she enthused.

The group mumbled a response.

"Is it still morning?" queried my neighbor under her breath.

"Let's try that again, good morning!" Another collective mumble.

Oh, boy, I thought, *tough room.*

I scanned the crowd one more time and then focused my full attention on Janice. I think I was more nervous than she was. Totally unfounded, as it turned out.

She began, "Before I give the microphone to Bob, I just want to take a few minutes to tell you why we're here." She paused. "No...let me tell you why *I'm here*. And, frankly, I almost wasn't.

"I joined this company because I believed in what we had, and I believed in what we had because Teddy Garrison painted such a compelling, awesome picture of the future. And in a very short time, his vision infected and inspired me, and I found myself not only believing in XinoniX, but also falling in love with it."

She looked around the room and, it seemed to me, made eye contact with all three hundred people.

"I would wake up every morning and literally jump out of bed. In fact, there were many nights I didn't go to bed at all. Nobody ever made me stay up all night to meet an important client deadline. Nobody ever made me feel like I'd be a slacker if I didn't push myself. The only person I ever had to answer to was myself. And although there were many times that I was really, really tired, I was never exhausted.

"Just out of curiosity," she said, scanning the crowd, "how many of you can remember feeling the same way?"

At least eighty percent of the hands went up, including my neighbor's.

"That's what I thought. And be honest, please. How many of you still feel that way?"

After a lot of shuffling and sidelong glances, four hands went up—reluctantly, it seemed.

"I, for one, thank goodness for the four of you, because as you may have noticed I did not raise my hand. And I'm supposed to be a leader. I've been thinking about this a lot, trying to figure out what went wrong for me."

She paused and looked down at her hands.

"I was really pissed off when Teddy left. I felt abandoned and betrayed by the very person whose vision I had taken as my own. I couldn't believe that everything we had worked for was so *meaningless* to him that he could discard us like a sack of trash. That's what it felt like to me. Was I the only one?"

Several shaking heads, many murmurs of no.

"It looks as though I'm speaking for many of you. And that may be true. But let me speak only for myself for a moment when I say that I've been a complete idiot. Not an idiot for believing in XinoniX, but for tying that belief to one person.

"Teddy was a great leader for us. No doubt. But he was not the be-all and end-all; he was not the ultimate factor in our success. In fact, that's exactly why he was a great leader, he built a company that could succeed without him; not because of him. When I realized that, it suddenly became clear exactly what had gone wrong for me. I'd forgotten one vital thing: this is *our* company, dammit."

Her face flushed.

"The people in this room developed and continue to develop our exceptional software, the people in this room sell that exceptional software, the people in this room take superb care of our clients, the people in this room—every one of us—can change the world if we want to. And I want to.

"Rumors have been circulating that I'm leaving XinoniX. Last week those rumors may have been true. But I'm here to tell you that I'm not going to leave. And I'm not going to stay only to go through the motions, collect a paycheck, and live my life on the weekends. As of today, right now, I recommit myself to our success and to the success of our clients. My energy is back, and I won't let it wane again. And, quite frankly, whether or not you choose to come along with me, I'm charging ahead. But I want you to come with me.

"Some of you may be thinking that, as an executive, I'm supposed to talk like this whether I mean it or not. Others of you may suspect that I'm making a calculated attempt to pump you up, to motivate the troops in a desperate last-ditch effort to save XinoniX. I might feel the same way if the roles were reversed.

"I'm not trying to change your hearts and minds; it's been challenging enough to change my own. All I can tell you is that I love this place and I love what we can become, and I am completely, unabashedly, and unapologetically in love with the kind of future we can create together."

The room was electric; I could tell she was getting through, and I damn near stood up and applauded. I opted for professional constraint.

Janice said, "I'm asking each of you to do only one thing for now. Ask yourself the same question I asked myself: why did you love XinoniX before, and how can you get that feeling back? If you can, then let's get about the business of making our distinct mark on the world. If you can't, then ask for help. I had to. I got my help from a close friend and confidant—"

Now my face flushed.

"—and from Bob Jeffers." She looked over at Jeffers, and he appeared genuinely surprised at Janice's comment. "And if you can't get that feeling back, and if you don't want to ask for help, then—and this is just the simple truth—it's time for you to leave and find your passion somewhere else. Life's too short; don't live it without your heart."

She stopped and let silence fill the room. Janice Everson had just revealed herself to her colleagues and done it magnificently. I knew there wasn't one single ounce of bullshit in that entire speech, but I wondered if the authenticity was as evident to the company as it was to me.

A hand went up. "Janice?"

"Yes, Sondra?"

"Was that an ultimatum?"

"Yes. Yes, I guess it was." The room murmured. "But it's exactly the same ultimatum I gave myself."

"Fair enough," said Sondra.

That was pretty good evidence that Janice had connected. Sondra was in. Sondra, who only minutes before had been known to me as Crap Lady.

25.

After a brief and sincere introduction from Janice, Bob Jeffers stepped up to the microphone. Whereas Janice had been confident and comfortable, Jeffers appeared awkward and even a little bit shy.

"I'm a little nervous," said Bob quietly into the microphone. "I think I have a reputation as a man of few words. It's not that I have nothing to say, or that I'm antisocial. Well, not entirely antisocial."

That brought a few tentative chuckles from the crowd. "It's just that I'm, well, more of a numbers guy than a words guy. So I hope you'll be patient with me as I try to, um, express myself to you. I do have something important that I'd like to say."

He cleared his throat.

"I'd like to say that I'm sorry. And I'm asking all of you to accept my apology."

After a short, awkward silence, someone from the middle of the room called, "What are we forgiving you for, Bob?" A few more tentative giggles followed.

"I appreciate that, but I think you already know.

"Look," Bob went on, "I may be a man of few words, but I do have ears. And I hear what people say about me. Nobody here has ever called me The 51% Guy to my face, but I have heard the name, and, believe it or not, I know where it came from. The infamous fifty-one-percent rule has been following me around for the past ten years. For those of you who may never have heard about it before now, let's just say that it comes from my reputation as a boss who believes he has all the answers and has to have the final say on everything. In other words, I always have to own fifty-one percent of the vote. I always have to have it my way. Command and control. Theory X management. Right? Does that describe my reputation fairly well?"

Some people actually had the guts to nod in response to that. I was impressed, given that Bob hadn't denied it was true.

"Well…it's all true. At least it *was* true. Through most of my career, I've seen myself as the big boss, the one with all the an-swers, and I was never really interested in other people's, espe-cially my *subordinates'*, ideas or opinions. If you worked for me, your input was useless. Unless, of course, it agreed with mine.

"Then, a few years ago, I had a pretty severe heart attack. Almost died. Instead of losing my life I was, thankfully, given the chance at a new one. That's when I realized that my whole approach to work and life had been unhealthy. It's unhealthy for me to act as though I have to control everything because I can't. Right? So I tried to do things differently. Tried to be more of a team player. I tried to be more inclusive. I tried that for about two weeks before I said, 'Screw it. Command and control *works* for me.'

"Then I met Teddy, and he invited me to XinoniX but on the condition that I change my management style."

This was news to me. From the look on Janice's face, to her as well.

"A condition that I accepted and then readily ignored. And that," he glanced at the fellow in the middle of the room, "is what I'm asking your forgiveness for. Janice made a commitment to you; I will as well."

For the first time since the meeting started, he looked over to me and ever so slightly raised his eyebrows as if to say, *Okay, here goes. OS!M time!*

"I am going to be more inclusive as a manager and more supportive as a colleague to each of you in this company. I am going to do my part to help us change the world. That's an audacious intent, but I believe that all of you—our team, our company— are capable of living up to it. And I want to be a leader worthy of the task and worthy of you.

"I don't expect all of you to believe me just because I'm saying these words. I still need to prove it to you and, over time, I will. So I'm asking that we start with a clean slate. That we start over. I'm not saying that we'll run XinoniX as a democracy, or that we'll all vote on every decision. That's no way to run a business either. I'm not saying that every decision I do make will be popular. I am saying that the fifty-one-percent rule is hereby abolished. And I am going to spend more time with all of you to hear your ideas and to understand your perspectives. Most important, I'm asking you to make your own decisions in your own areas of responsibility. You know what it takes to do a great job around here. I trust you to do it.

"Oh, and one more thing." He stepped away from the microphone and fumbled around in his briefcase, while Janice watched with curiosity. This, obviously, hadn't been planned.

He pulled out a lime green folder and handed it to Janice. "I think this is yours," he said. It was her marketing plan.

26.

With the top down in the Mustang, I drove away from XinoniX and headed for home, my mind lost in what I'd just witnessed. I marveled at how, in just a few minutes, the mood of an entire company had shifted toward the north. People had stayed in the cafeteria long after the meeting adjourned talking to each other and lining up to offer their congratulations and support to Janice and Bob. They had both publicly pursued very personal OS!Ms. Now all they had to do was follow up on their commitments and continue to prove their words through their actions. I knew they would.

I don't know how it happened exactly, but I soon found myself pulling the car up to the curb in front of Pops's trailer. I noticed the roses had been recently trimmed and petals scattered on the doorstep. Probably just the wind's doing, I thought. I walked up to the door, picked up a scarlet petal, and gazed at it as it fluttered gently in the palm of my hand. For some reason, I thought about Smitty and realized that this moment was rife with significance. I was lost in a reverie of rich symbolism when the door swung slowly open.

In spite of myself, I ran through the doorway and gave the freaking brat a mighty bear hug.

"I'm...I'm...so sorry for your loss," I stammered. I've always been lousy at the grief thing; I've never known what to say to those left behind.

"It's okay, dude," he said quietly. "C'mon in."

Boxes were scattered around the trailer in various stages of being packed and taped. We walked out to the yard and sat in the same chairs we'd shared with Pops only a few days earlier. Sunshine sparkled down through the jasmine and cast speckled shadows on the porch.

"We've known for quite a while that it was coming," said Edg. "We just didn't know exactly when."

"But he looked so vibrant," I said. "I never would have guessed there was anything wrong with him."

"That's probably because he was ready to go; he'd come to terms with it. What you saw was a man deeply at peace with what he'd done with his time on this planet."

Edg took a deep breath that quavered slightly and caught momentarily in his throat. "I miss him like you wouldn't believe," he said. "And it's only been a day."

"Of course I believe it," I said. "He was your Pops." I decided not to pry about funeral or memorial arrangements; for some reason, it didn't seem appropriate. "What about your mother?" I asked instead.

"She died shortly after I was born."

"I'm sorry," I said, flustered.

"Not your fault. Besides, Pops more than took up the slack. I never lacked for love and guidance."

"Any brothers or sisters?"

"Nope. Just me and the old man."

We sat in silence for a few moments until Edg abruptly switched gears. "I'm glad you stopped by before I left."

"What do you mean?" I asked, trying to sound calm. "Left for where?"

He laughed, which oddly didn't seem at all inappropriate, even under these circumstances. "I'm gonna take care of Pops's stuff, make a few of the necessary arrangements, and then I'm outta here. I need to get away for a while. It's time for a long overdue surfing excursion. Big waves await me at other shores."

"Wait a minute," I said. "I feel like we've just gotten started." That sounded grossly selfish, I knew, but I didn't care. It felt like a great and valuable friend was about to slip away from me, so I launched into a quick description of what had just gone down at XinoniX. I told him how he had inspired me and how I had been able to use his insight to help Janice and Bob.

"XinoniX already feels like a new company," I said. "But I know there's so much more to do. Don't bail on me now, Edg," I pleaded. "I mean, we've only scratched the surface of LEAP, right?" I noticed myself getting desperate, and I didn't like the feeling.

He answered me with a broad, classic Edg grin. "Wait here," he said. "I've got something for you."

He jumped up and bolted into the trailer. I leaned back in my chair and stared up into the deep blue San Diego sky. An enormous pelican coasted overhead toward the ocean.

"Hey!" he said, snapping me out of my trance. "I want you to have this." He slapped a small, glossy notebook down on the bistro table. I looked at the cover. It had a pale blue background with bold black letters that said,

A Daily Handbook for Extreme Leaders:
How to Do What You Love in the Service
of People Who Love What You Do
By William G. Maritime and Son

"With this," he said, "I'm sure you can take it from here."

"You and Pops wrote this together?" I asked.

"More like we lived it together. We just did our best to capture the essence of Pops's approach to life and work. Tried to make it real simple."

"Did you publish it? I've never heard of it before," I said as I reached to pick it up.

He smiled. "That's the only copy."

I jerked my hand back as though I suddenly noticed a rattlesnake on the table. "Whoa! I can't keep this. This is yours, Edg. You'll regret giving it away; I can't let you do that."

"Well, that's mighty thoughtful of you, buddy. But why don't you just take a look inside before you decide to pass." I picked it up and flipped through the pages. It didn't take long. There were only a handful of them.

"Not exactly *Grey's Anatomy*, is it?" he chortled. "So you can believe that I have it committed to memory, right? It looks really simple, but I guarantee, dude, if you use these pages, it'll keep you on course. *Use these pages every day, and I swear to you, you'll never stray.* Pops and I came up with that. It was our own little jingle."

"All right," I laughed, "I will. But not because of the jingle, I want you to know."

"One more thing, Steve. Pops and I always meant this to be a living document. We knew it wasn't really done, that there'd always be more to put in. So, I'd like you to do me a favor, if you wouldn't mind."

"Anything, Edg. Name it," I said without hesitation.

"As time goes on, as you continue to grow, to learn, to get into and out of trouble…"

"Sounds like me."

He smiled. "I'd like you to add your thoughts to this book. Farber-ize it. Make it yours, too."

I was honored, of course, but mostly just flat-out stunned. I squirmed.

"I'm not sure that's gonna happen, Edg. But if I really think I have something to contribute, I will. And only because you asked me to."

"Thank you. You're a good man, Mr. Steve. I'm happy to have known you."

"Wait, wait, wait a minute!" I exclaimed. "I'm not quite ready to say good-bye here. I've just got one question for you, all right? It's a little thing, but it's making me nuts. Will you grant me just one last question, oh great, wise, and mysterious Edg? Okay?"

"Okay. Sure. As reward for your acerbic sarcasm. Go ahead."

"Okay," I said, mentally rubbing my hands together like a little kid. "What's the story behind your name? It's gotta be a nickname—but for what?"

"Well," he said with a little smirk. "It's kind of a contraction between my first and last name: Ed G."

"But," I started tentatively. "Pops's last name was Maritime, so yours is, too—right?"

"Pops's last name was the same as mine, but it wasn't Maritime. Not really."

"What?"

"Pops had a great sense of humor, that's what."

"Huh?"

"When I was a kid, I loved the comic book *Richie Rich*. All the characters' names were a reflection of who they were. Richie Rich was, obviously, rich. Lotta was big, remember, as in a whole lotta girl?"

"Yeah? So?"

"So, when I was about eight, Pops started his boat leasing business."

"Yeah?"

"*Maritime*, dude! He went by the name of William G. Maritime. It just stuck. G is the first letter of his real name, and, of course, mine too."

"Get outta here!" I cried. "You can't be serious! What a hoot!"

"It's been our private joke for almost all my life. Now you're in on it, too, and I expect you to protect our sacred secret," he said with mock gravity. At least I think it was mock.

"Okay, then," I said, "so what's the G stand for?"

"Really, Steve," he said, "you're kidding, right?"

"What do you mean?"

"You know what it stands for."

Yeah. I guess I did.

Later On

27.

The plane was coming in for a landing over Grand Rapids. I looked out the window at the Midwestern landscape that spread out below us like a beach of light white snow. On to the next gig: a four-day executive off-site session where I would be holed up somewhere in the wilds of the Michigan countryside with fifteen senior managers of a manufacturing company. Odd as it might sound, I was genuinely jazzed at the thought.

Several months had passed since I'd said good-bye to Edg at Pops's trailer. I had tried to see him one more time before he left town. I'd driven back to Point Loma, back to that stately Tudor home with the ivy and stained glass window. This time, I'd bounded boldly up to the door and rung the bell. This time, I'd pounded on that door when no one answered. And this time, the door to the home of Teddy Garrison had finally swung open.

Sadie leapt through the doorway, jumped up, and licked her wet tongue across my face. "Down, girl! Mind yer manners!" he called from inside. "You'd make for a lousy watchdog, I'll tell ya that."

And with that, Smitty the Sign Reader stepped up to the threshold.

"Well, hi, hello, how are ya?" he said when he saw me standing there. "C'mon in and take a load off, Mr. Farber." I followed Smitty to the back of the house and into the informal dining area off the kitchen. I could see the gazebo through the beveled windows. Two cups of coffee sat steaming on the cherry wood table.

"Nah, I ain't no psychic. I didn't know you were comin.' I already have company is all. Here, have a seat, and I'll get you a mug." He walked into the kitchen.

The bathroom door opened and Janice walked in, pulled up her chair, and sat next to me.

"Hi there," she said, leaning over to give me a hug. "So, you found him."

"Uh-huh. So did you, apparently. Why didn't you just tell me where he lived?" I asked, feigning annoyance.

"I don't know. It was too obvious. I'd already looked for him here with no luck."

Smitty delivered my coffee and sat down across from us. We all looked at each other.

"Well," he said with a cowboy grin, "here we are!"

"He's gone, isn't he?" I asked.

"Yep," said Smitty. "Mr. Ed 'Teddy' Garrison has done vamoosed to whiter shores and bluer waves. I'm lookin' after the place while he's gone. Which, by the way, could be quite a while."

Ed "Teddy" Garrison. Edg, the son of Pops Maritime. Surfer, businessman, philosopher, friend, and advisor. It had all come together for me when I had held the two notes side by side and seen the striking similarities in the handwriting. The kind of similarity that's often there between father and son.

"So, by the time you had asked me to look for him," I said to Janice, "he had already found me."

"Sure looks that way," she said.

"So he engineered this whole thing," I said sounding more annoyed than I felt. "He approached me knowing that you and I were close, and that I would ultimately use his guidance to help you. I can't believe it."

"He didn't use you, Steve, if that's what's bothering you."

She was right, of course. Edg had said in the beginning that I'd be doing him a favor, that we'd be helping each other. If Janice had known I was hanging out with Garrison, she would have been so caught up trying to get him back that she'd have blown her opportunity for greatness. And if I had known, I'd have felt like a middleman, and I really wouldn't have learned a thing. And the value of what I learned was absolutely immeasurable.

"Aw, well, who the heck knows?" quipped Smitty. "Maybe it was all just a happy coincidence."

"Hey, Smitty?" I said.

"Yeah?"

"Read the signs, man." I said it so it sounded like *sahns*. I stood up in front of the executive team and handed out the materials for the off-site meeting. These folks were engineers, mostly, and predominantly male. Good, salt-of-the-earth, no-nonsense, hard-working human beings who ran a company of five thousand people fitting the same general profile. We had worked together before, this team and I, so they could tell right away that something was different. The last binder that we had used contained around 250 pages of text, quotes, and worksheets. Once they returned to work, it made for a great doorstop. This one had thirteen pages.

"Okay, folks," I said, "let's get started. Here's the operative question for you and your company: How are we going to change the world?"

A Daily Handbook
for Extreme Leaders

How to Do What You Love in the Service of People Who Love What You Do

William G. Maritime and Son

Cultivate Love

Love is the ultimate motivation of the Extreme Leader: love of something or someone, love of a cause, love of a principle, love of the people you work with and the customers you serve, love of the future you and yours can create together, love of the business you conduct together every day.

Think about it...
Without the calling and commitment of your heart, there's no good reason for you to take a stand, to take a risk, to do what it takes to change your world for the better.

Think about it...
You take your heart to work with you every day, and so does everyone else—everyone, that is, who falls into the general

category of human being. So, think about it. Right now. Answer the following questions for yourself. Take some time; think it through. Once you're clear on the answer, tell people. That's right, you need, ultimately, to answer these questions out loud—and often—to the people you aspire to lead.

> *"Why do I love this business, this company?"*
> (Answer out loud, please.)

> *"Why do I love this project, this idea, this*
> *system, this procedure, this policy?"*
> (Answer out loud, please.)

> *"Why do I love my customers?"*
> (Answer out loud, please.)

Then answer this question, not with words but through your actions:

> *"How will I show that love in the way I work with,*
> *serve, and lead the people around me?"*

Here's one of many ways to do that:

WRITE A PROFESSIONAL LOVE NOTE.
At least once a day, write a personal, handwritten note of appreciation, thanks, or recognition:

Think about a specific person at work.

List that person's finest qualities and/or greatest achievements.

Reflect on why you appreciate those qualities and achievements.

Write the note.

Give the note.

Make it a habit, not an assignment. In other words, always write from your heart and express your sincere appreciation. The note bridges words with action. You're demonstrating love through the act of writing and delivering it.

But don't do this because you have to; do it because you want to.

So, want to.

You are now in the business of cultivating love. And watch, just watch, how love comes back to you wrapped beautifully in the words and actions of others.

The bottom line: Love is good business. Customers who love you will return to you, your product, your service, and your company. Employees who love you will bring themselves fully into their work day after day, no matter that the company down the street is paying a bit more.

Love is your retention strategy.

So, how do you get them to love you? Simple, really,

Go first...
or don't bother calling yourself leader, let alone Extreme Leader.

Generate Energy

> Energy *n.* **1**: internal or inherent power; capacity
> of acting, operating, or producing an effect
> **2**: strength of expression; force of utterance;
> power to impress the mind and arouse the
> feelings; life; spirit
> —*American Heritage and Webster's dictionaries*

The Extreme Leader is a generator, a powerful force for action, for progress, and an enthusiastic believer in people and in their capacity to do the awesome.

What gets you out of bed and brings you into work? If you are to be the generator, where does your juice come from? In what well do you dip your cup to get the nourishment you need to meet the obstacles and challenges that you and yours face every day? Find out and go there often.

Make a list of your personal energizers and encourage others to do the same.

The answers are different for each of us, certainly, but there are some universal sources of energy that are available to all.

Don't worry, this isn't esoteric; it's not metaphysics—not that there's anything wrong with that.

So, what generates energy?
Love

Great ideas

Noble principles

Leaping goals

Interesting work

Exciting challenges

Compelling vision of the future

That's a pretty good start. If you're doubtful, consider the opposite: Imagine working at a place you hate, a place that squashes ideas, ignores principles, sets goals you can accomplish in a coma, provides boring work, provides no challenge, and has no idea where it's going in the future—actually, it doesn't matter that they don't know where they're going, because a company like that will never get there anyway.

Feeling energized yet? Of course not. For you, the Extreme Leader, the ultimate test will be:

> *"What effect does my action have on the energy of the people around me?"*

Experiment with some of these:

Remember/discover why you're here.

Are you just filling in time between weekends?

No? Then answer this:

> *"What is your work really all about? What is your higher purpose?"*

Tell people. Ask them for their help in living up to that purpose. Encourage great ideas from people.

Never assume that an idea is stupid just because it sounds that way to you. Your response: Go try it. If it doesn't work, ask:

"What's the lesson for you and us?"

STAND ON PRINCIPLE; WORK FOR A CAUSE.

Principles and values are there to guide your actions and decisions. They are the standard. But consider this:

> The Extreme Leader doesn't just meet the existing standards; she or he defines higher ones.

So...

"What are your noble principles and values?"

Nail them on the wall. Tell everyone, everywhere you go:

"This is what's important around here. Judge me by my ability to live up to them."

Now you're working for a cause, not just a paycheck.

SET LEAP GOALS.

Your goals should require that you leap and experience OS!Ms to meet them, not stretch, as some have said. A leap goal will require you to get excited and energetic if you're going to make it. Set goals that tap into the talents, skills, hopes, and aspirations of your team and company, and people will generate the energy necessary to leap up and hit those goals.

> *"What goals can you set for your team and your company today that will tap into the talents, skills, hopes, and aspirations of your people?"*

PURGE THE SUCKERS.

Get rid of the energy suckers. Encourage people to root out and discard any work that hinders your cause.

Ask yourself; ask your people:

> *"What are the unnecessary, time-consuming, bureaucratic policies and procedures that suck our energy?"*

> *"What are we doing that keeps us from fulfilling our and our customers' goals and dreams?"*

> *"What should we change in order to make this a more interesting, exciting, scintillating, and awesome place to work?"*

CONNECT HUMAN-TO-HUMAN.

Communicate yourself, your humanity. Don't just recite your company's vision statement. Talk in your own words. Talk to people about your ideas for the future, and ask for theirs. Be the person that you are.

Forget your title, forget your position, and speak from your heart.

Talk not only of your hopes for the future but also about your foibles today. Vulnerability aids human connection, and connection is the conduit for energy. Pretense of invincibility builds walls and creates distance between human hearts.

"What keeps me from achieving Frequency more often?"

"What pulls me out of Frequency?"

Inspire Audacity

For the Extreme Leader, audacity is a bold and blatant disregard for normal constraints in order to change the world for the better. Love-inspired audacity is courageous and filled with valor. The Extreme Leader is audacious not to serve his or her own ego, but to serve the common good. And to do so boldly and blatantly and let the naysayers be damned.

Watch out...

The most common and insidious normal constraints are the ones that are imposed on you by others. This imposition is not malicious, necessarily. It just comes from a sad, limited set of beliefs about what's possible.

DON'T LET THEIR BELIEFS BECOME YOURS.

Normal constraints take many forms. Whenever you have an idea, whenever you see a better way to do things or better things to do, make a list of all the normal constraints that seem to be holding you back. Are they systems, policies, or procedures? Is it a particular person or group of people? Do you doubt yourself? Is your company's history holding you back? Many audacious ideas and actions have been thwarted by the simple words: "We tried that once, and it didn't work then," or "That'll never work around here; it's just not the way we do it," or "You're dreaming."

Now, for the all the right reasons, disregard that list!

And then ask and answer the following question. It is the ultimate audacity question because of its scope and extraordinary possibilities. *It is impossible to be an Extreme Leader without putting this question at the center of your agenda*:

"How are we going to change the world?"

You can tackle that by thinking, literally, about the entire world, the global community. And bless you for thinking that way. By the same token, however, it is no less noble to ask and answer this question:

"How are we going to change the world of our company, employees, customers, marketplace, and industry?"

Remember, the entire world is made up solely of people like the ones you touch in your personal and professional life. So, why not start with your world? Every normal constraint in the proverbial book will tell you that this question is unrealistic and a waste of time. Boldly and blatantly disregard that book.

Now ask others to join you in this endeavor. Show them what you think is possible, and show them that your belief in their capabilities is greater than their belief in their own. Ask others to help you to change the world and you have just inspired audacity.

Provide Proof

Are you really an Extreme Leader? Prove it.

Prove it through the alignment between your words and your actions. Prove it by standing up for what's right. Prove it through measurable, tangible signs of progress. Prove it through your own experience. Prove it through your phenomenal successes. Prove it through your glorious failures. And prove it all on these three levels:

  Prove it to others.

  Prove it to yourself.

  Prove to others that you're proving it to yourself.

Prove it to others.
It's been called a lot of things over the years: *walk your talk*; *practice what you preach*; *put your money where your mouth is*; *set the example.* Jim Kouzes and Barry Posner said it best: DWYSYWD. Dwi-zee-wid. Do What You Say You Will Do.

Whenever humanly possible make sure that your actions and behaviors live up to and reflect the words and ideas, promises, and commitments that come out of your mouth.

Ask yourself:

> *"What have I done today that shows my
> commitment to my colleagues and customers?"*

> *"How have I changed the World/world, even a little bit,
> today? What measurable, tangible evidence can I provide?"*

> *"What will I do tomorrow to demonstrate
> the power of my convictions?"*

Prove it to yourself.

The OS!M is the natural, built in indicator that you are quite possibly fully engaged in the act of Extreme Leadership. Pursue it, it's your internal barometer that you're moving in the right direction. This is not about fear for fear's sake; it's not about the adrenaline rush just for the thrill of it. This is about the fear and thrill that are part and parcel of the leadership experience. It's the fear and thrill that we experience in the process of attempting the awesome, the extraordinary. It's how you prove it to yourself. There is no Extreme Leadership without the OS!M.

Do you think you've empowered someone? Did it scare you? Did you have an OS!M as you thought about what that person might do with his or her newfound discretion? If not, you haven't pushed it far enough. Increase the scope of the empowerment until you feel it in your gut, even if you have to push it to a million-dollar spending authority. Feel the OS!M now? Good. That's growth.

Reflect…

> *"What are the OS!Ms in my past that resulted in my*
> *being where I am today? What lessons did I learn*
> *in those OS!Ms that I should continue to apply?"*

And if you could do them over…

> *"What would I keep the same in spite of a particular failure?*
> *What would I change in spite of a particular success?"*

Now…

> *"What potential leadership opportunity is*
> *coming up at work or at home that I can turn*
> *into my next OS!M? How will I do it?"*

Prove to others that you're proving it to yourself.
Extreme Leadership is not a solo act; it doesn't happen in a vacuum. You're not going to change the world by yourself. It's your job to recruit, cultivate, and develop the Extreme Leaders in your midst. This is nothing new. You've heard it before: develop people. True, true, and true again.

However…

The most overlooked way to develop Extreme Leadership in others is to let them participate in your development. You be the living, breathing example of a work in progress.

That's what we all are anyway, right? Say to them, "Watch me try." Give others the benefits of your OS!Ms.

That's right...

Pursue your OS!Ms in full, public view.

Show others that you're learning, you're trying, you're botching it up from time to time. Then let them in on what you've learned.

Guess what will happen?

They'll try, too. You've proven to others that you're proving it to yourself. They'll want to prove it to themselves, too.

But don't leave it there. Invite them to share in your development directly.

Seek extreme feedback. Ask these questions:

> *"What do I need to do to improve as an extreme Leader?*
> *Where am I screwing up? How can I get better?"*

Don't give up until you get their answers—until you've proven that you mean it.

Your Radical Leap

A Self-Assessment for Extreme Leaders

1 — Strongly Disagree
2 — Disagree
3 — Neither Agree nor Disagree
4 — Agree
5 — Strongly Agree

Survey Statement	Circle One Number for Each Statement				
1. I hold myself to a higher standard than I expect from others	1	2	3	4	5
2. I take action and risks that are needed to make things better	1	2	3	4	5
3. I demonstrate a clear confidence in the skills and abilities of the people around me	1	2	3	4	5
4. I consistently demonstrate that I am doing the work I love	1	2	3	4	5
5. I stand up for what is right	1	2	3	4	5
6. I create an environment where people can change the world that is within their reach	1	2	3	4	5
7. I share the vision of the future that makes people want to get fully involved	1	2	3	4	5
8. I am passionate about the work and the people I lead	1	2	3	4	5
9. I have clear alignment of word and action	1	2	3	4	5

Survey Statement	Circle One Number for Each Statement				
10. I enjoy situations and actions that are scary and exhilarating at the same time	1	2	3	4	5
11. I inspire others to do their best	1	2	3	4	5
12. I am highly motivated by the work and the people who support this work	1	2	3	4	5
13. I accomplish goals and deliver results	1	2	3	4	5
14. I do things to support the team even when it is not popular	1	2	3	4	5
15. I explain the higher meaning and purpose of the work in ways that energize others	1	2	3	4	5
16. Through my actions and words, I inspire others to love the organization, the team, and the work	1	2	3	4	5
17. I show measurable and tangible signs of progress	1	2	3	4	5
18. I help others overcome their fear of change	1	2	3	4	5
19. I give others work that is challenging and rewarding	1	2	3	4	5
20. I help people see how they can do something significant and meaningful	1	2	3	4	5
21. I follow through on commitments and promises	1	2	3	4	5
22. I find ways around the normal constraints to change the world for the better	1	2	3	4	5

Survey Statement	Circle One Number for Each Statement
23. I help others see the link between their work and the work of the overall organization	1 2 3 4 5
24. I spend time to help others develop as leaders	1 2 3 4 5
25. I inspire courage in others so that they can take purposeful risks for continuous improvement	1 2 3 4 5
26. I recognize and celebrate others' creative efforts even when those efforts result in "failure"	1 2 3 4 5
27. I help people find the work that they love doing	1 2 3 4 5
28. I show a genuine caring and interest in employees and customers	1 2 3 4 5
29. I demonstrate a commitment to make things better even when there is a risk of failure and sacrifice	1 2 3 4 5
30. I use my own mistakes, errors, and failures as an opportunity for learning and for teaching others	1 2 3 4 5
31. I remove or change unnecessary policies and procedures	1 2 3 4 5
32. I form teams of individuals who share the love for the work, the team, the organization and the organization's customers	1 2 3 4 5

Your Radical Leap Results

Your Personal Ratings of Love, Energy, Audacity, and Proof

Copy your results into the grid on the next page, or you can simply enter your scores at www.LeapAssessment.com for a free read-out of your personal ratings in the categories of Love, Energy, Audacity, and Proof. Or, scan this QR code:

Cultivate Love

Statement number	Your Rating
4	
8	
12	
16	
20	
24	
28	
32	

Total Score for Cultivate Love:

Generate Energy

Statement number	Your Rating
3	
7	
11	
15	
19	
23	
27	
31	

Total Score for Generate Energy:

Inspire Audacity

Statement number	Your Rating
2	
6	
10	
14	
18	
22	
26	
30	

Total Score for Inspire Audacity:

Provide Proof

Statement number	Your Rating
1	
5	
9	
13	
17	
21	
25	
29	

Total Score for Provide Proof:

The Extreme Leadership Saga Continues!

Read on to begin your journey to *The Radical Edge* by Steve Farber.

The Radical Edge

Another Personal Lesson in Extreme Leadership

Steve Farber

Prologue

I was stuck deep in the wilds of Michigan, in the middle of winter, on the back end of a raging snowstorm that had left the countryside covered in—what do poets like to call it?—"a downy soft blanket of white." That sounds much nicer than "a blinding, frozen wasteland," which is a much more accurate image. I wasn't exactly stranded out on the tundra, however, I was holed up in a toasty conference room inside a quaint but efficient bed and breakfast built for the burgeoning corporate off-site market. Moreover, I wasn't alone because I was facilitating an executive retreat for, and I mean this in the nicest way, a roomful of middle-aged, white guys named "Jim."

Blatant gender and ethnic homogeneity aside, this was a group of very intelligent, dependable, and steadfast mid- to senior-level managers of a large Cedar Rapid–based manufacturing company, and I was an experienced and newly re-energized leadership consultant on a mission. The group was thrashing around trying to come to terms with a question that I had just dropped on them like a sack of salt on the road-way. It wasn't the kind of question that they teach in facilitator school—such as, for example, "Who would like to volunteer to jump out of a tree?"— but a question that demanded the group look at their role and their company's role from an entirely different perspective. A question that required a very deep level of thought and reflection as well as a steroidal dose of intellectual and moral courage, and that reflected my new perspective on the nature of meaningful life and work in the twenty-first century:

"How are we going to change the world?"

Apparently, it was a question that invited the inner cynic frothing with spittle and ablaze with venom to emerge, as well.

"Are you kidding me? What kind of question is that?" raged Jim.

"Ummm, a really important one?" I offered.

"How is that supposed to help me with my ridiculous work-load, Steve? I mean, c'mon."

"Look," said another Jim. "I think it's a good question. I think we should be willing to consider it at least. It'll make for a good discussion, anyway." Several Jims nodded in support.

"Hold on," said Cynical Jim. "I don't think this is just about having a discussion." He looked at me. "I'm assuming that you don't want us to just talk about how we're going to change the world, you want us to do it. Am I right?"

"Yeah. That's about right."

"One question for you, then, Steve."

"Okay."

"Assuming that we spend the time on this instead of the other really important questions that we need to address at this meeting, and assuming that we actually come up with an answer—"

"Good assumptions," I encouraged.

"Okay, then here's the question I'll want answered. What, exactly, does a person like me need to do to make it all happen?"

"You mean what do you personally have to do to change the world?"

"As long as we're asking the deep questions, yeah."

"And another thing," said another Jim. "We do have a business to run here. Are we just supposed to forget about that while we're out changing the world?"

"Yeah," said yet another, "not to mention having something resembling a personal life in our spare time."

I paused. I looked out the window. I looked back at Jim. I opened my mouth. I closed it again. These were damned good questions.

I wished I had the answers.

A WUP Upside the Head

1.

I live in the Mission Beach area of San Diego, California. It's a bit different from Michigan, especially in the wintertime, and I was desperately trying to get back there after my conference with the Jims. There are no direct flights from Grand Rapids to San Diego International Airport, unless you had enough cake to hire your own personal jet, which, of course, I didn't. I was prowling the sleek metal and glass halls of O'Hare and killing time as I waited for my connection, which was delayed for an unspecified amount of time. I had ignored the gate agent's admonishment to "remain comfortably seated in the boarding area" in case the weather gods suddenly changed their game plan. The airline was having enough trouble negotiating their pilot contracts let alone getting cooperation from the supreme powers that be, so I bugged out to wander the concourse and pump a little blood into my travel weary brain cells.

I had a lot to think about. The meeting had gone okay, I guess. They had all left thinking much bigger thoughts than what they'd come in with, and I felt really good about that. A shift in perspective is no small thing, to be sure, but I was feeling the dull ache of regret—or was it discontent?—that I used to get after teaching the canned, scripted workshops that were the staples of my earlier days in the leadership development business. Don't get me wrong, I loved the idea of changing the world as the core business and leadership proposition, but I still found myself doubting my ability to actually get it done. I didn't want people to mention the names of Don Quixote and Steve Farber in the same breath. Tilting unabashedly at windmills is one thing; slaying dragons is a whole 'nother smoke.

I turned a corner and found myself face-to-face with a large and very odd billboard advertisement. It was a picture of a blue Oxford button-down shirt with a red power necktie, and it would have been the classic image of clean, conservative business, if not for one bizarre detail: the tie was on fire. Accompanying it was a big, bold headline that read, "Burn Your Boss" and a tagline at the bottom that said, "Report the use of unlicensed software." This was, essentially, an invitation—no, a challenge— for a person to spy on and rat out their management, and it was punctuated with an 800 number hotline for people to *call right now* and strike the sparkling, gratifying match of revenge.

Now I have as much respect for intellectual property rights as the next guy. Probably more. I'm not a fan of pirating or plagiarism. I sided with Metallica over the early Napster debates and will gladly pop for a buck a song to download to my iPod as opposed to trolling the web for free sources. Software's in the same category, especially on an enterprise level. However, "Burn Your Boss?" Have things really gotten that bad? Did these people honestly expect to tap into some unexpressed reservoir of rage trembling under the surface of other business travelers like myself? More importantly, was this ad working? There was one way to find out. I called the number.

I was hoping to get a live person on the line so I could simply ask the question. What I got, though, was a recorded message saying something about their organization and their office hours followed by an invitation to leave your information—about that evil boss, I assumed—after the tone. As to the question of whether their ad was working, I got my answer right away. Before I could say anything, their machine spoke to me. It said, "You cannot leave a message because the mailbox is full."

2.

I shoveled the gobs of mail from my box, punched in the security code on the front door, and climbed the two flights of stairs to my apartment overlooking Mission Bay. It was always strange to return home to an empty perch and see how much dust had managed to accumulate on the kitchen counters in just one week. The sea air mixed with fine sand always found its way in with or without the security code.

Like scratching for gems in a litter box, I sifted through the mail—junk, bills, a belated birthday card from my dentist, a check from a recent client project—and threw the whole pile on the round oak kitchen table. There was one item that looked a bit more personal, so I picked it up for closer inspection. I tore open the envelope to find a delicate, handcrafted note card from my friend, Janice, who was a grand high muckity-muck at a local bio-tech company. Janice and I were old friends, and I had recently helped her out of a sticky career jam. The handwritten words inside the card offered a friendly thinking of you kind of sentiment followed by a postscript reading,

I've given your name to my friend, Rich Delacroix,
CEO of Independence Lending Group. He may be call-
ing you for a coaching engagement. He's a nice man.
Please don't hurt him.

She followed it with one of those endearing little emoticons to indicate that she was smiling about that last part.

I rooted around in my empty kitchen but no amount of persistence was going to uncover anything resembling food. As I headed back out the door for a Jack in the Box run, my cell jangled a funky electronic tune.

"Steve Farber?" inquired the voice on the other end of the line. "This is Rich Delacroix. Janice gave me your number. I know this is short notice, but do you, by chance, have time for a quick visit to my office?"

Here in the 21st century, the archetypal call to action mostly comes via the digital phone. Jack, I thought wistfully, would have to wait in his box a little bit longer.

Independence Lending Group, Inc.'s (ILGI) snappy commercials promising the best mortgage rates and fastest service on the planet were plastered all over the television and radio airwaves. Maybe they were true; all I knew was that the company had grown like gangbusters during the nuclear boom in the real estate market and the feverish refi activity fueled by subterranean interest rates. I'm usually not impressed by people who make fortunes in bull markets, even though, come to think of it, I never have, but this was one of the few mortgage companies that also managed to survive the subsequent economic meltdown. And that was noteworthy.

ILGI's corporate offices were in La Jolla's University Town Center (UTC) neighborhood. UTC is a cement and glass amalgam of apartments, office buildings, malls, restaurants, and a Mormon temple that keeps an impressive and watchful eye over the endless traffic on Interstate 5. I parked my Mustang in the visitor's parking structure and took the elevator up to the eighteenth floor. The receptionist announced my name into the phone, and before I had a chance to settle into a plush leather chair, Rich Delacroix came bounding through the door on the far end of the waiting area. He was young—mid thirties, I guessed—tan, fit, blond, energetic and, although his attire was casual, exceedingly well dressed.

Despite all that, I liked him immediately.

He gripped my hand with an unsurprising firmness and ushered me into his corner office with a dramatic view of the Mormon temple. I got lost for a moment in the symbolic possibilities.

"Steve," he said. "Thanks so much for taking the time to come over. I know you're a busy man with a lot on your plate. So let's get down to it, okay?"

He walked me over to a small conference area in the corner of his corner office, and this time I did sink down into a beautiful, rich, brown leather chair.

"Happy to help if I can, Rich," I said. "What is it that you need?"

"Me, personally? Nothing." I raised my eyebrows, and he hesitated for a moment. "I don't mean it to sound that way, I'm not perfect...that's not what I mean. But I have a very weak link in my management team, and he's the one that really needs help— or that I need help with."

It was really rather endearing to see this supremely self-possessed individual squirm as if he had a tapeworm.

This was not a dude who was used to asking anyone for help, let alone a virtual stranger.

"Okay, lay it on me," I said taking out my yellow legal pad. "Give me the whole story."

3.

Closer, dealmaker, phone demon, top producer, Cameron Summerfield is a sales god. He came to work at ILGI fresh out of state college where he'd graduated unceremoniously with a liberal arts degree. Armed with a diploma on the wall and the money bug up his butt, he finagled an interview at the exploding mortgage company and, of course, nailed it. He raced through training and attacked the phone with the enthusiasm and compassion of a taunted pit bull, setting a record for new loans in a single month in the first month of his career. His third month on the phone yielded a commission check of eighty thousand dollars. That's not a misprint, and it was no fluke. Cam was golden week in and week out. He bought a loft in downtown San Diego, a Blaupunkt sound system, and a Porsche Carrera. He was twenty-six years old.

Now he was the youngest senior vice president in the history of the company. His promotion, it was beginning to seem, being Rich Delacroix's big mistake. The problem, apparently, was really pretty simple: the salespeople, who all ultimately reported to Cam, hated his guts with a steaming passion. Turnover, which was already high in the mortgage industry, was through the roof, and ILGI's best sales talent was bailing at an alarming rate.

"Why? What's he doing that's so despicable?"

"Look," Rich said. "Don't misunderstand, I happen to like Cam very much, and there's no doubt that he's an extraordinary salesman, but leadership doesn't come as naturally to him as closing deals. I want him to make this work, but he's flat-out brutal with the sales team. I'm a believer in incentives and disincentives, too; I like a little friendly competition among the team. But he takes it all too far."

"I'm going to need you to be more specific, Rich. I could interpret that in all kinds of ways. I mean, brutal is a pretty strong word. He's not, like, jamming wood splints into the soles of people's feet, right? So what does Cam's brutality look like?"

"I'm not going to tell you that right now."

"Really? Why?"

Rich pointed over my shoulder and I looked back as the door swung slowly open. "Okay to come in?" called a voice from the hallway.

"Give us a few more minutes, Cam. Be right with you." The door shut with a quiet click.

"Oh. So you just want me to dive right in, huh?" I paused for a second before continuing. "Tell you what, Rich. I don't really know if I can help or not, but I'll make you a deal. Starting tomorrow morning let me hang out with Cam for a day or so, get to know him a bit. If we hit it off you can start paying me. If we don't get along, we'll part ways and I won't send you a bill."

"Sorry," he replied. "I'm a little confused. You want to hang out with him? What does that have to do with coaching?"

"Do me a favor," I said. "Go over to your computer and Google executive coach." He remained seated, staring at me. "C'mon. Humor me."

Rich walked over to his desk, typed the words on his keyboard, and hit return.

"How many hits?" I asked.

He raised his eyebrows. "3,520,000."

"Add another seven hundred thousand or so for leadership coach and 130 grand for management coach and you get the picture, right? Listen, Rich, there are a lot of great coaches out there and some very fine coaching associations and curricula available to those who want to learn how to coach. But anyone can hang out a shingle on the Web and spend an hour a week on the phone with a client, and any one of them would be more than happy to work with Cam."

"Okay..."

"I won't, though, unless..."

"Unless what?" Rich interrupted.

I shrugged. "Unless I like him."

4.

I was flying once from New York to San Francisco after conducting a workshop in which I'd talked nonstop for two straight days. Now I'm not saying it was two days of sparkling verbal gems, mind you, but talk takes energy and mine was gone. Cashing in my first-class upgrades and relaxing in total, blissful silence with a good novel was what I desired the most. Golden ticket in hand, I stood in the boarding line and watched as they loaded up the families traveling with small children contingent. Inching toward the Jetway, a young woman dragged her squirming little boy by the hand. He wailed and howled at the top of his lungs as though she were tearing off his little digits one by one.

Having traveled with my own kids when they were little, I know how stressful a fussy child can be for the parent. Just as I was thinking how difficult this flight was going to be for the young mom, this guy standing in front of me yelled, "*I knew it! I knew it!* I heard that kid screaming in the terminal and I said, 'that kid's gonna be on my flight!' *I knew it.* It never fails!"

What a jerk, I remember thinking. That poor woman was feeling bad enough already. She needed this jerk's vociferous commentary as much as she needed a rabid hyena strapped to her leg.

A few minutes later I walked on the plane and to my horror I realized who my seatmate was: The Jerk. I felt like screaming I knew it! Every time there's a jerk on the plane they end up next to me! But I didn't. Instead, I sat down, buckled up, pulled out my book, and locked my eyes on the pages. I sent out megatons of don't talk to me vibes and felt confident there was no way he would dare to reach through my pulsating, death star force field. He couldn't possibly have the gall to...

"Hey! Waddaya reading? Oh! I read that book! I've read everything by that guy! Do you live in Frisco or are you going there to work? Man, am I glad I'm not sitting next to that *kid*. Did you hear that kid screamin'? Hey! Waddaya wanna drink?" He waved a hand in the air. "Waitress! They hate that, har-har-har! We are ready to start *drinkin'*!"

This situation is what's known in behavioral psychology circles as a lost cause, so I closed my book, accepted the drink, resigned myself to several hours of pressurized cabin torture, and threw myself at the mercy of the verbose and soon to be plastered Jerk Man. Funny thing is, I had a great time.

Sure, Jerk Man was a bit over the top. He was too loud, and, yeah, he had the emotional intelligence of a bottlenose fly, and I don't mean that in a judgmental way, but he was interesting, eccentric, and a gifted raconteur. In short, by the time we landed in San Francisco, I was glad I'd met him.

"Pretty funny," said Rich. "I assume you're telling me this for a reason?"

"Yeah. Of course. Let me ask you a question with a ridiculously obvious answer. Why was Jerk Man talking to me?"

"What do you mean?"

"I mean why was he talking to me and not the guy sitting back in 10C?"

Rich furrowed his eyebrows. "Ummm...because he was sitting next to you?"

"Right. I was strapped in next to him and not going anywhere for several hours. We talked and got to know each other for one simple, profoundly obvious reason: I was there."

"Okay," mumbled Rich, still not seeing my point.

"Proximity. Physical nearness. Face-to-face and shoulder-to-shoulder, Rich. That's the only way to really connect with another human being because that's the only way we really get to know each other."

"And that's why you want to hang out with Cam."

"And that's why I want to hang out with Cam."

"Okay, I get it, Steve. One question, though: after hanging out with Cam, talking with him, getting to know him, what if you don't like him? Does that really mean that you won't work with him?"

"I wouldn't worry about that."

"Why?"

I grinned. "Because I like everybody."

5.

Rich punched a button on his phone and a few minutes later Cam threw the door open and sauntered into the office. He looked like—how can I say this nicely—a cocky *GQ* wannabe. He wore tasseled loafers, wool pants with razor-sharp pleats, a silk shirt, and enough hair products to slick a porcupine. He may as well have been wearing a sign saying, I make money. I really do try to resist snap judgments, but my first thought, I have to admit, was *Danger, Will Robinson!* I stood up and shook his hand as Rich made the introductions.

"So," said Cam as he gave me the once-over, "I understand you're going to give me some of the latest, cutting-edge sales techniques. I'm all ears for anything that'll keep me on top of my game, dude."

I looked at Rich. "Sales techniques?"

He flushed. "Well, Cam, that's not exactly what I had in mind by inviting Steve to work with you."

Cam stiffened as if someone had just stuck a live wire down his Armanis. "What do you mean?" The question caught in his throat. "What's goin' on here?"

"I'm more of a leadership coach, Cam. Extreme Leadership," I said in a Bond, James Bond sort of way. "Rich has asked me to help you get a handle on leading your sales team."

"Why?" he asked, shooting a look at Rich.

"Look, Cam," Rich began. "It couldn't hurt for you to expand your skills in that area. We all know that you're the man when it comes to selling. No one's going to argue that point. But... you've got to get your leadership act together if you're going to be a part of this company's future. Don't act as if this is a total surprise. It's not like we haven't talked about this before, right?"

Now it was Cam's turn to flush. I watched the redness rise from his neck to his ears to the top of his forehead. *Thar she blows!* I thought. Then as quickly as his skin had erupted, the color dissipated and he regained his composure.

"Okay, sure, fine. Whatever," he huffed. "When do we start?"

"Tomorrow morning," I said.

"And what do we do first?"

"We have breakfast."

6.

The morning was gray and overcast; the kind of day that gives June Gloom its name. This was December, however, and the Mission Beach coastline was doing that water and sand thing without the slightest inclination or care about what my day was going to be like. I don't know why I love gray beach days. Maybe it's because they make me look differently at the pounding waves and squawking seagulls. The birds and the waves don't care if the sun's out or not. That's not a bad attitude for a human to adopt.

Just before the north end of Mission Beach turns into Pacific Beach, Mission Café abuts the boardwalk. You can get a cup of coffee and a muffin and sit right outside where the action is. Cam and I found a spot at a table behind the short retaining wall that separated the porch from the boardwalk. I took in a full, deep breath of sea air. Man, what could be better? My morning coffee, steaming and potent; the Pacific, rolling and churning; the beach walkers, strolling and talking, all of it reminding me— not that I needed it—of how much I loved this place. The air smelled of suntan lotion, which told me that despite the cloud cover, the early morning crowd was characteristically optimistic.

I'm always amazed by the variety of earnest morning walkers: college kids clipping along in their baseball caps, cargo shorts, and tight-laced Adidas, older folks glad still to be walking at all, skaters on their boards, and bikers riding backwards on their handlebars. It's quite a parade—not the kind that would have inspired John Philip Sousa, but I never really cared for his music anyway.

All this I kept to myself. Cam, however, was more external with his thoughts than I was. I slowly realized that he was spewing forth an endless stream of color commentary on the overweight, over-thin, over-plasticized, over—or under—whatever of every person passing by. He didn't realize it, but he was pushing my buttons as rapidly and aggressively as a rat beeping a scientist for food. It didn't sound like anger so much as condescension, arrogance, and an overall *these people suck* perspective on the scene.

"Jeez! Look at *that* guy. Can you believe him? He looks like a dog I used to own. Get a load of that hair. What a fleabag!" He gave me a conspiratorial nudge on the arm. "What sewer did he sleep in last night?"

The current object of Cam's attention was, indeed, a little scruffy looking, I suppose. He was tall and wiry, and his too-tan arms poked out from the cutoff sleeves of a blue tie-dyed T-shirt. Green khaki cargo shorts and Reef flip-flops completed what was a fairly run-of-the-mill beach ensemble. However, it was his amazing hair that set him apart from the rest of the crowd: prolific red dreadlocks fell down from the top of his head, and, beginning just beneath a wide, prominent nose that held up round, lemon yellow sunglasses, a giant, red mustache and beard stuck out in all directions at once. As if on cue, the sewer dog in question launched himself over the retaining wall, scooped up a chair, and swung it over to our table. He sat down next to Cam and across from me as though we'd been expecting him all along. Truth was I had. If our visitor's unruly, red beard really had been casting off fleas, Cam's mouth would have caught them all.

"Here's the funny thing, Cam," I said, enjoying his shock. "This fleabag here is a friend of mine, and, it just so happens, he's our breakfast date." I could feel my smile broadening as I watched Cam digest this bit of news.

Smitty grinned at Cam and then bear slapped me on the back like he always did. "Farberoni, my man, it's a great day to be alive and kickin', especially considering the alternative." Smitty's laugh is infectious. It starts somewhere deep down in his body and seems to ripple all the way to the ends of each red hair—and that's a lot of rippling. Cam, however, looked as if he was afraid of other infectious things.

"Smitty, I'd like you to meet Cam; Cam, my friend Smitty here is one of the wisest people I've ever met, and I'm not embarrassed to say so."

"And I ain't embarrassed to hear you say it. It's a pleasure, Mr. Cam," Smitty said, extending his tan, weathered hand. Cam shook it without much exuberance, but Smitty wouldn't let go. He gripped Cam's hand as if he was trying to squeeze a marble out of a fish. "Dang, son! You look a lot peppier than you are." Smitty leaned in close to Cam and whispered, "You been drinkin' your milk?"

Cam's face reddened and he squeezed back.

"Don't get angry now, son," said Smitty. "I'm just messin' with ya. Now why don't you order me a coffee, here, Farberama. And get this boy a glass of moo juice. I'll be right back. The lizard's barkin', if you know what I mean." He jumped up and ran off to find the public terrarium, if I knew what he meant.

"What the hell was *that* all about?" hissed Cam. "Are you really expecting me to waste my time like this? I thought you were supposed to be coaching me." He said *coaching* like he was trying to eject something nasty from the back of his throat.

I gazed out at the water and calmly replied. "Listen, Cam. Give Smitty a chance; you may be surprised what you can learn from him. Appearances aren't always what they seem, right?"

"Wait a minute," he said in amazement. "I just thought that he was your friend. Are you trying to tell me that he's here to help me? This is a joke, right?" He waited for me to answer. "Right?"

Smitty returned much faster than I'd thought possible, but there he was parking himself next to Cam and cozying in nice and close.

Cam leaned back in his chair. "What is this?" he said looking over at Smitty. "*A Christmas Carol*? When do I meet the ghosts of breakfasts past and future?"

Well, well! Cam has a sense of humor. I had to admit I was impressed by his joke, despite the spiteful tone.

"Something bothering you, son?" said Smitty. "Is there something you wanna say to me?"

"Yeah."

"Well go on, then."

"Stop calling me son."

"Sorry, Buck. I don't mean nothin' by it. Just a Texas habit. So tell me a little about yourself."

"Like what?" Cam said with a sniff.

"Well, for starters: where'd you go to school?"

"San Diego State. Graduated with a degree in Sorority Relations and I was immediately brought into ILGI where I decided pretty damn quickly to take no prisoners. Four years later, I'm twenty-six, I'm senior vice president of a mortgage company with over a thousand people on the payroll, and it's up to me to make sure we're closing deals and writing loans. And I've got my boys and girls whipped into shape." He popped his sleeve over the enormous watch on his wrist.

"All right, then. You like to read? Read any management stuff?" Smitty asked, as he started mixing half a dozen packets of sugar into his coffee.

Cam raised his eyebrows at the empty sugar packets collecting one by one on the table. "I don't have time to read books that tell me what I already know. Not to sound arrogant or anything but I've got, like, instinct or something. You can't teach that. I can smell a deal. All I need is that feeling, and…BAM…another client for the company and money in my pocket. And, by the way, it's not chump change I'm talking about."

"Well, Buck, I'll bet you just about got it all, then— the Porsche, the kick-ass apartment in the city, designer clothes, martinis at The Bitter End, steaks at Donovan's, and more bling for your many young ladies then they could wear in a year. That about right?"

"That's about right, *Buck*." Cam said proudly looking my way. "Can we go now? I've got a sales team to run."

"Now hold on a minute, there, Buck!" hollered Smitty. Several people at other tables looked our way to see what the fuss was about, and Smitty instinctively lowered the volume on his Texas boombox voice.

"Just relax," he said quieter. "You're getting the wrong idea. You're thinkin' that I'm some kinda money's-the-root-of-all-evil kinda guy. That I'm gonna tell you that the pursuit of material things is shameful. And that you're a shallow, shallow little boy."

Cam shrugged indifferently. "I don't really care what you think of me, to tell you the truth. But, yeah, that's what it sounds like, and I don't need a lecture in ethics. There's nothing wrong with the way I live, so butt out."

This was not going quite as well as I'd hoped.

"Smitty," I interrupted. "Fair's fair. Since you're giving Cam the third degree, why don't you tell him a bit about your background?"

"You betcha. Happy to oblige." He turned to Cam. "Ever hear of a little company called Maritime?"

"Maritime and Son? Sure, who hasn't?"

"I was CIO."

About the Author

Steve Farber is the Founder and CEO of The Extreme Leadership Institute, an organization devoted to helping its clients in the business community, non-profits, and education to create award-winning cultures and achieve radical results.

Former vice president and official mouthpiece—that's what it said on his business card—of legendary management guru, Tom Peters Company, Farber is a seasoned leadership coach and consultant who has worked with a vast array of public and private organizations in virtually every arena, from the tech sector to financial services, manufacturing, healthcare, hospitality, entertainment, retail, public education, nonprofits, and government.

He's the author of *Greater Than Yourself: The Ultimate Lesson of True Leadership*, which debuted as a *USA Today* and *Wall Street Journal* bestseller; *The Radical Leap: A Personal Lesson in Extreme Leadership*, which was named as one of the 100 Best Business Books of All Time; *The Radical Edge*, which was hailed as "a playbook for harnessing the power of the human spirit"; and *Love Is Just Damn Good Business*, published by McGraw-Hill in September of 2019.

He lives, as you may have guessed, in San Diego.

WORK WITH STEVE FARBER AND THE EXTREME LEADERSHIP INSTITUTE TEAM

Listed as one of Inc's global Top 50 Leadership and Management Experts, Steve Farber is a leadership pioneer, strategist, keynote speaker and bestselling author on Extreme Leadership. His expertise is in creating organizational cultures where leadership is not just an opportunity and obligation for those in authority, but for everyone at all levels.

His accessible, deeply inspirational, and eminently practical Radical LEAP framework is widely used across the business, non-profit and education spectrum. Farber has been credited with redefining leadership in deeply personal yet practical terms and re-energizing thousands of people to make a significant difference in their businesses, personal lives, and the world around them.

Farber's Extreme Leadership Institute team develops their programs with one thing in mind: radical results for their clients. As a result, they have helped more than 20 companies achieve "Best Place to Work" status.

Steve and The Extreme Leadership Institute team can work with you by:

- Delivering practical, inspiring and entertaining keynote speeches
- Operationalizing LEAP in your business to earn a competitive advantage
- Embedding the practices of Extreme Leadership in your organization's DNA
- Providing significant on-going leadership learning and development

- Creating and amplifying deep employee engagement
- Developing your award-winning culture
- Helping you to achieve radical results

Steve has worked with or spoken to hundreds of organizations large and small in virtually every industry--from the tech sector to financial services, manufacturing, health care, hospitality, entertainment, public education, retail, and government. His clients include such notable organizations as American Greetings, Intel, TriNet, Hyatt, Ernst & Young, Qorvo, and BNI.

To book Steve Farber for your next event visit
www.SteveFarber.com

To learn about The Extreme Leadership Institute's full offering of consulting, coaching, and training services, visit
www.ExtremeLeadership.com

Take the LEAP assessment online and receive lots of great resources too at **www.LeapAssessment.com**

BRING THE EXTREME LEADERSHIP WORKSHOP TO YOUR ORGANIZATION

Develop Extreme Leaders throughout your company or team with The Extreme Leadership Workshop. This highly adaptable workshop is designed as a one-day (8-hour) workshop but can be tailored to 4 hours or extended to 2 full days, depending on your specific needs. It is facilitator-led and includes individual reflection and action-planning, small group interaction, and built-in videos featuring author, Steve Farber, explaining and applying the Extreme Leadership concepts. It also includes a series of exclusive, follow-up videos from Steve to keep your participants on the path to Extreme Leadership.

Become Certified to Teach The Extreme Leadership Workshop. There are only a handful of certified, licensed, Extreme Leadership Workshop facilitators on the planet, and you now have an opportunity to be one of them. In this powerful and transformational workshop, you'll explore the key tenets of the Extreme Leadership Framework—Cultivating Love, Generating Energy, Inspiring Audacity, and Providing Proof—and learn how to apply them to your personal and professional leadership challenges. And then, with personal coaching from Steve Farber and his team, you'll be given all the tools, resources, and experience you'll need to facilitate this workshop for others.

At the end of the program, you'll be licensed to offer this unique workshop to your clients, your company, your team, your colleagues, or your community; just as important, you'll become part of our exclusive facilitator "tribe." For more information email **info@ExtremeLeadership.com** or call us at **858-513-4184.**

CONNECT WITH STEVE FARBER!

facebook.com/stevefarber

/stevefarber

@stevefarber

@Steve Farber